D0878972

IRRESPONSIBLE

AND

MALADJUSTED

IRRESPONSIBLE AND MALADJUSTED

ESSAYS

WALTER CUMMINS

Del Sol Press
Washington, D.C.

Irresponsible: and Maladjusted: Essays
by Walter Cummins

Published by Del Sol Press
Washington, D.C.

All rights reserved. No part of this book may be reproduced or transmittted in any form or by any means, electronic or mechanical, including photocopying, recording, or by any information storage and retrieval system, without prior written permission from the publisher, except for the inclusion of brief quotations in a review.

Copyright © Walter Cummins, 2020

First printing 2020

Cover: Peter Selgin

Printed in the United States of America

ISBN 978-1-7344900-0-8

Great thanks to Renée Ashley, who—in addition to her many achievements as a poet, reviewer, and essayist—is a master editor.

Thanks to Martin Donoff for encouraging me to write and rewrite an essay about my arrival at FDU.

Thanks to Alison Cummins for proofreading and for advice of forty years.

To the memories of my father, mother,
brother, and sisters,
with thanks for enduring my youth

ACKNOWLEDGMENTS

Initial versions of these essays appeared in the following publications:

"My Father in the Attic," *The Doctor T.J. Eckleburg Review*

"Pin Boy," *The Doctor T.J. Eckleburg Review*

"High School: The Bleak Years," *The Literary Traveler*

"Existentialism and Absent Father," *Eckleburg 21*

"The Military-Industrial Complex and Me," *The Del Sol Review*

"The Way the World Works," *Trouvère*

"What We Really Do," *Writers on the Job*

"How I Became a College Professor," *Serving House Journal*

"Moonlighting," *From Pantyhose to Spandex: Writers on the Job Redux*

"Willliam Zander, 1938-2019," *The Literary Review*

"Beardless in Mississippi," *Serving House Journal*

"Trolleyology," *Arts & Letters*

"The Day Robert Graves Sang to Me," *The Literary Traveler*

CONTENTS

LIVING IN MY PAST

THE THEORY THAT YOUR LIFE FLASHES before your eyes in the instant before you die is one I'll be testing in not too long, considering my advanced age. But I have a question. For the dying person, does what is an eye blink for everyone else become an extended experience, a slow-motion iteration of all that happened from one's emergence from birth canal to the last gasps of mortality? Some sort of Einsteinian elongated space-time phenomenon? I'm skeptical. My inclination is to expect a high-speed blur before the transition from being to nothingness.

That's why, while I still have time, I'm taking this opportunity to linger on my past in these essays, recollections of incidents and events. What follows is certainly of questionable veracity, distorted by the flaws of memory and the groping for appropriate words. If that final life-flash actually happens, I'm sure it—in contrast—would be flawless.

Such a life-flash might even have meaningful continuity and tell a coherent story of my existence, one that's beyond my understanding. The best I can come up with are fragments, a gathering of random events, primarily examples of inadequacy and folly, many still as embarrassing now as they were at the time they occurred. But at this stage of my life, I'm immune to shame. After all, what can they do to me that I haven't done to myself?

As a dyed-in-the-wool existentialist, I accept that existence precedes essence. Who we are at any moment varies with the decisions we've just made. As the years piled up, I've had to make many. They've had the effect of being unwanted tests. Some I failed, others I passed, usually by the skin of my teeth, blundering into adequacy, my "I" in ongoing flux, a work in progress—or regress.

One consistent trait has been my inclination for irony, which translates into an inability to take myself all that seriously. Even in the midst of the worst moments, I'm unable to suppress a comic perspective that, when the event fades into memory, serves as a source of laughs. My mother called me a *smart aleck*, a polite term for smart ass.

In our final months of high school, we seniors were required to write a 250-word autobiography, which led to choruses of outraged grumbling. So many words, my classmates muttered and cursed the unfairness of it all. My self-story ended up being facetious, a prototype for the many thousands of words I've written since. To begin with, I claimed I had been hatched by aliens, which I now realize is an analogue for having a mother and father old enough to be my grandparents. But not then. Then I couldn't take the assignment seriously. Yet teachers passed mine around, whispering about me, shaking their heads. They didn't get the joke. Or, perhaps, I was the joke.

If I could go back in time and redo that assignment, I might offer two extremely embarrassing examples about the four-year-old who was once me. The teenagers on my street decided to put on a show in one of their backyards, constructing a stage and setting up rows of folding chairs. I don't recall their acts, probably too terrified to pay attention, but I was supposed to climb up the wooden steps and recite "Mary Had a Little Lamb." Standing in the spotlight and looking out at the faces of the assembled neighbors, all people I knew and, much worse, who knew me, my mouth clamped shut. I panicked and ran home around fences and through yards, parents in pursuit. My guess is that the audience was amused. I, a pathologically shy child, was humiliated.

I suspect anyone who had seen that show, even the teenage performers, is no longer with us. I'm probably the only one who remembers. But even more embarrassing from that age and recorded forever on photographic paper for the world to see is the group pose of my preschool class at Miss Coon's for-a-fee kindergarten. The four-year-old me stands smack in the front row wearing short pants, one hand grabbing my crotch—blatantly. My assumption now is that I had a full bladder. But why that reaction at the moment the camera snapped? Why wasn't the photographer kind enough to warn me? Did he want to show the print around for laughs? One more thing to be ashamed about, tacked prominently on the wall of memory all my life.

In the most recent photograph I've seen of myself, almost eighty years after kindergarten, I'm standing with both hands firmly and safely on a lectern, reading to an unseen audience beyond the edge of the picture, my head fringed with white hair, the visible side of my face covered with a white beard, my expression content, a universe away from running off the stage.

And at that moment I was actually happy, no longer morbidly shy, no longer the reticent observer off in a corner taking mental notes, too timid to raise my hand. Over time I've plunged into the thick of things, willing to reveal my blunders and stupidities, ongoing misdeeds of that hapless kid with his hand on his crotch. At least, that's the way I see it. The vicissitudes of existence rather than any inkling of an essence. Still, the chronicle that finally flashes before my eyes may reveal something else entirely.

Author's Note: The pieces in this collection were written over a number of years as stand-alone essays. Certain incidents have been repeated as information necessary for a particular piece. Apologies for the redundancies.

FLEEING THE CLASSROOM

THE WINDOWSILLS WERE CLOSE to the floor in my first-grade classroom, an easy climb even for an uncoordinated, scab-kneed six-year-old. I remember that much so many years later. But it's one of my few memories. I certainly have no idea what led me to hop up to that sill, duck under the open sash, and run home. I did that several times, with home just a few blocks away. For some reason I didn't want to be in school. My mother dragged me back. Did she yell? Did I cry? No idea. Whatever punishment ensued it didn't stop me from fleeing the next time.

And it wasn't just that beckoning, open window. A few times, the window closed, I ran out the classroom door in the middle of a lesson, Mr. Holtznagle, a gaunt janitor in coveralls, summoned to catch me under my arms and carry me back.

Our grammar school was a model of poor design. You couldn't get from one end to the other without going through other classrooms. I must have bolted from the first grade into rows of startled second- or third-graders, spreading the disruption. Were the other teachers and other kids stunned, or did they just yawn and think, Oh, it's him again?

As far as I know, I was the only kid in all eight grades to bolt from the classroom, which I suppose is a certain distinction. Others did talk to me on the playground. I wasn't shunned. Did anyone bother to ask me why I was doing it? Or did they just assume that was the way I was? The weird misfit.

The teacher didn't punish me, beyond a sigh. Perhaps my flights provided a diversion from her mundane ABC days. Perhaps a pool in the teachers' room—when would he do it again? Dollar bills tossed into a kitty. I still have a sense that my teacher—Miss Warneker, I believe—was a very nice woman, one who liked tiny kids, their malleable innocence.

Another, but very different first-grade memory. During a play break, all the others digging into a toy chest for their favorites, I chose to sit at my desk with a piece of lined paper and write each number from 1 to 100. By happenstance, that was the lesson plan's first afternoon assignment. Miss Warneker didn't know what to do with me—once again. She shrugged and told me I could just play with the toys. I had them all to myself, amused to my heart's content while others toiled.

That experience had a profound impact on my approach to education years later. In graduate school, I kept up with assignments and wrote my term papers midway through the semester. While others in the days before finals were up half the night in frantic scrambling, I could sleep peacefully and even earlier in the evening enjoy the equivalent of a toybox.

My fleeing didn't last. A deportment notation on

my third-term report card said, "Walter has improved greatly. Gets along very well now."

In fact, beyond that mere "improved" I did a complete turnaround and ended up spending decades of my life in classrooms, happy to be there. I do recall some of my students cutting, dozing, leaving the room early—but none escaping out a window. In that I consider myself unique.

MY FATHER IN THE ATTIC

Oh quickly disappearing photograph
in my more slowly disappearing hand
—Rilke, "Portrait of My Father as a Young Man"
(trans. Stephen Mitchell)

AMONG THE CLUTTER IN OUR ATTIC, unpacked through
the twenty years since we moved into this house, rests
a large framed photograph of my father taken when he
was twenty-nine, or so I've been told. That photograph,
about twenty-four by eighteen inches, leans against a
beam, shrouded in black plastic and sealed with strips
of masking tape. It was wrapped that way long before it
went into our attic. I don't remember who had it before
me, most likely my late sisters. And I can't recall the last
time the photograph hung on a wall, perhaps before I
left for college decades ago.

Yet, despite my not actually having seen the picture
for so many years, I remember it clearly. It's more fixed
in my memory than my father himself. He died suddenly
a month before my eighth birthday. I was in bed early
one morning, not yet up for school. He was in the bathroom shaving; then a loud thud and a clatter. Screams
of my mother and sisters, men of the local ambulance
squad thumping up the stairs. No chance of resuscita-
tion. Probably an aneurism of his heart or brain. My

mother didn't want an autopsy. The last I saw of him was a shape strapped onto a stretcher.

My recollections of our interactions are slight, mainly the products of what others told me we did together—movies like "Lassie," wooden bleachers to watch our town's semi-pro baseball team, nickels for ice cream at the diner next to the shop where he repaired and custom-made shoes. (I still can visualize the four-inch lift he made for a man with one leg significantly shorter than the other.) The only event I really recall is a time when I was six. My friend H.D. and I were so pleased with ourselves for sticking pins through the outer skin layers of our fingers. We ran into his shop to show him. He feigned being impressed and opened the cash register for a reward of ice cream money.

When he died, he was sixty-two. In January, 1944, the month of his death, he had achieved the average life span for an American male at that time. I, now his only surviving child, have enjoyed many more years, even beyond today's average, thanks to diet, exercise, and modern medicine. Had he survived and lived on, he would be one hundred and thirty-six now.

He was in his mid-fifties when I was conceived, my brother and sisters already grown. I've had this imagined conversation for quite a while, my father moving close to my mother in their bed and whispering, "What could happen at our age?" Little did he know. The joke was on them. Although a pregnant woman in her forties today would barely get a second glance, it was a rarity

back then, a bit embarrassing even though my parents
had been long married. Probably the notion of people
so old doing it. Their ages made me feel different, odd,
people assuming my parents were my grandparents.

My sense of my father in his final years comes from
two black-and-white snapshots, one in which he stands
in our yard in a white shirt and dark tie, hands at his
side, looking straight ahead, suggesting a tension at being photographed. He wore rimless glasses, was bald
expect for a thin fringe back from his temples, a small
man, trim. The other snapshot was taken during a parade, my father in a row of men, an air raid warden's
insignia wrapped around his upper arm. He was, I've
been told, very proud of his role in World War II, at a
time my brother was an army first lieutenant in Europe.
I played with metal toy soldiers, demolishing Nazis with
comic book exclamations.

But in the attic photograph, my father was still not
yet thirty, probably with a newborn son, my brother.
The photograph, tinted with color, seems meant to function as a portrait, my father posed in a three-quarter
profile, his expression serious, though not grim. What
stands out most for me is the full head of thick wavy
hair, impressively coifed. At twenty-nine I had a bald
spot at the crown of my head, an earlier start than his;
but eventually he was much balder than I've ever been,
though I'm clearly a bald man.

How could I have really known my father? He was
gone before I reached an age when serious conversations

would have revealed his thoughts and experiences to me firsthand. But for most of my life, while they were still alive, my siblings told me how much he and I were alike in quirks and disposition. Nature over nurture.

I lack enough sense of his disposition to make a judgment. Perhaps his amusement at the pins through my fingertips is a clue. I tend to regard the world with an ironic shake of my head. Did he? I do know he was an obsessive reader. In one oft-told tale he was supposed to be minding my then-young siblings one evening while my mother was with friends. She came home long after their bedtimes, finding house lights ablaze, kids still playing, my father engrossed in a book. Sounds normal to me.

Beyond the tendency to live in our heads through books, he and I share political and travel inclinations, along with an aversion to military service, a very different burden from being an air raid warden. As a young man in Eastern Europe, when borders were so fluid it's hard to identify the then-country of his origin, he fled to escape conscription, an act I associate more with a press gang than a letter from the draft board. I didn't leave my country but took the easy way out through six months active duty in the National Guard, never advancing beyond private E-2. On the other hand, my brother, his first son, left active duty as a Captain, retired from the reserves as a Lt. Colonel, so committed to the military he was buried in Arlington Cemetery wearing his officer's uniform.

My brother's politics were fixated on the super-patriotic right. Like my father, I lean left, proud that my heritage involves a man who spent part of his twenties as an organizer for Eugene V. Debs. Supposedly in the 1930s, he and my brother got into frequent shouting matches over political issues, several of which I must have overheard while in my crib.

Yet my father and brother shared manual dexterity and fine motor control that I sadly lack, even though my lefthandedness comes from my father. He could design and execute those special shoes. My brother became a podiatrist and performed surgical manipulations on people's feet. I wince when taking out a splinter and, if given the opportunity, probably would have mutilated a shoe or a foot.

My father, I was told, could function in a dozen languages, perhaps because of his travels through various countries to reach America. I get by in English. He was, I have no doubt, highly intelligent, my mother no slouch herself, producing a son and daughter who were high school class valedictorians and another daughter who was salutatorian. I, his second and last son, blundered my indifferent way into graduating with low honors.

But what could his intelligence have done for my father in the first half of the twentieth century when opportunities for smart people were so limited? I think of him in a category with the fathers of many of my college friends, men no doubt as bright or brighter than their offspring, who worked with their hands or ran small shops because there was nothing else for them to do, certainly not the executive positions or professional roles that their sons—and occasionally daughters—filled.

Perhaps my father was content to be self-employed and ease the walking of those with malformed feet, and then come home to read more books and lose himself in political musings.

The portrait photograph seems inappropriate for such a man, the self-important flaunting it suggests. Its existence always puzzled me from the time I was able to wonder. It couldn't have been cheap considering the size and the frame, and our family never had money for frivolities. Was it my father's idea? That doesn't seem like him, such a seeming display of vanity. Was it a gift? If so, from whom?

And why wasn't there a similar picture of my mother, equally large and equally framed? His must have been taken around 1910, a time when family photographs were coming into vogue. In them, the husband-father sat pompously in a chair, while the wife and children stood behind. I can't see my father sitting for such a pose or not being embarrassed to see his face hanging on a wall.

Now, of course, the picture doesn't hang, hasn't hung for years. It's up in the clutter of our attic amidst suitcases, a clothes rack, boxed documents, unused comforters, rolls of wrapping paper, bows. And it's unlikely that I'll ever unwrap it again.

As we contemplate downsizing, preparing for the time we won't need a multi-room house or have the energy to care for it, I wonder what will become of that picture. We'd already donated a few hundred CDs now that we have access to endless online music. We will donate our books, the hundreds I'll never have time to read again. Someone, somewhere still cares about all those authors.

But my father's picture? Other than me, there is not another living human being who ever knew him, who would get a frisson of recognition from looking at his face. Even I possess only the vaguest sense of his hand touching mine as he placed a coin for ice cream.

I wish he had lived long enough for me to learn about him—the books he read, his youthful travels, his ideas about the world. I have no doubt he would have interested me a great deal, and I'm pretty sure I would have taken great pleasure in our time together.

Once I'm gone, which will be sooner rather than later, my father will become one more totally forgotten being, one of the many millions who once existed since the first homo sapiens. His name exists in some record-ed census documents, evidence that there was once such a man. But to what end? The few remaining images of him will be meaningless to anyone who happened to see the man depicted.

But, aside from official facts and figures, no one will know his real history—what he did, where he went, what he read, what he thought, what he felt. People from the past we do remember—a tiny fraction of all who ever walked the earth—did something significant or infamous. A few have written memoirs that still matter. If my father had, the interesting bits would have accumulated before he sat for that picture—the escape from a brutal army, travels through Europe, romance with my mother, recruiting for Debs. Post picture, for all those years as a husband and father, his life sounds routinely mundane, though I hope it gave him satisfaction.

Better to leave the picture portrait wrapped in black plastic. Opening it wouldn't release the person. I'd certainly learn nothing new to add to the little about him I do know. Abandoned in an attic, removed from the world, sealed into darkness—the way of all our destinies.

MY MOTHER IN THE ATTIC

HERE'S JUST ONE VERY EMBARRASSING example of flawed memory. Imagine my chagrin when I went against the commitment I made in "My Father in the Attic" and unwrapped what I assumed was the framed photograph of my father stored amid the clutter under the rafters. We were downsizing, selling our home of more than twenty years and moving to a small apartment. Much stuff to jettison, much that would be hauled off to a dump. We distressed over objects we would have to abandon, the many memories they embodied. To my relief, a daughter interested in family history really wanted that picture of a man long dead before her birth. I carried the black plastic wrapping down to a bedroom, pulled off the tape, lifted a frame from the black wrapping, and—to my shock—stared at what had to be my mother's face. After a fumbling panic, I found my father's picture stacked behind hers. How could I have not known hers existed?

To the best of my now very suspect recollections, my mother's picture had never been displayed on a wall of any home during my youth. That could have been because my framed father honored a man who no longer existed, a reminder of his absence from the family. My mother was a constant presence during the years I lived at home, there in the flesh. But the person in the photograph looked nothing like the woman I'd known. It showed a girl of twenty, already a wife to a man ten years older, her clear-eyed square face under a covering of thick, dark hair. If I hadn't been aware of the picture's place in that wrapper, it could have been anyone; I wouldn't have recognized her. The mother I knew wore rimless spectacles on a plump face, her thin gray-haired strands pulled tight against her head and knotted in a bun.

That's the way she looked when she gave birth to me in her mid-forties. I know that from a photograph of her holding a baby that was me, she already gray, already plump. I was told the sudden turn to gray came shortly after that attic portrait photograph was taken, when she was pregnant with my brother and his still-born twin. In those days, at least in her case, a woman had to carry one dead fetus until the natural birth of the survivor. That carrying poisoned her system, turning her hair, destroying all her teeth for a lifetime of dentures. It may have been the reason for her weight.

I was not quite eighteen when she died, ten years after my father, her husband, she no longer plump but gauntly emaciated and in great pain, retching and vomiting from the intestinal cancer that killed her. While my father's death had been instantaneous, hers extended through weeks of agony. In the final hours she had a vision of her own parents at the foot of her bed.

From what she told me during my teens and what

my siblings added later, I knew much about the circumstances of her life, but little about what she was thinking and feeling beyond all the fussing to bake and cook and clean the house, going out now and then to meet with friends who always addressed each other as Mrs. This and That, never by first names. People did like her. My friends liked her, some even coming to her for advice that they followed. I took her for granted, too wrapped up in my teenage angst to appreciate all that she was doing for me, just assuming the food on the table and the clean clothes in my dresser were my right, something a mother simply did.

But for her, what was it like to be a widow, to have a son in a war, to have another surprise son arriving when she thought her family was grown, to put up with that son who was a brooding underachiever? And how much was she haunted by her own childhood? I knew facts, never emotions.

She had been born in Poland, one of several children, her mother dying when she was six, her father remarrying a widowed woman with her own children who would not have anything to do with his. My mother and her siblings were passed from relative to relative, all in poverty, she having to earn money as a child and help care for a younger brother. Were she and the others constantly hungry? Were they cold in winter? Did they wear more than rags?

Certainly, she was one of many of her generation who cherished her opportunity to live in America, even though our family scraped by. Still, she had a house to live in, furnishings, clothing, food, a family, essential security.

How she escaped the bleakness of Poland and got here, I don't know. If she ever told me, I don't remember. I do know she came with a sister we occasionally visited. Another sister was turned away at Ellis Island because she was blind. I have no idea of what happened to the brother and any others.

My mother was sixteen when she arrived in America, finding work rolling cigars in a factory in Richmond, Virginia, a job she did talk about. It was there—according to my sisters—my father saw the young girl running up and down a hill in a small park and told people that she was the one he would marry. I've seen that hill and the small brick house she lived in nearby. That was a while ago, the house, empty and boarded, one of a desolate row, now demolished.

When writing about my father in the attic, I speculated why there was no partner photo portrait of my mother, puzzled that my father would be so selfish, wondering where the money came from for that indulgence. I'm happy they shared the extravagance, though I can imagine the mother I knew fretting about the expense. Perhaps, though, that young woman allowed herself the frivolity, newly in love, at a peak of her life's happiness.

There's so much I don't know, even when I think I do.

AT THE AGE OF SEVEN

THE NIGHT IN 1969 American astronauts landed on the moon, I kept my daughter awake, excited at the event, more exited at the notion of providing my child a historic memory to transmit to her potential children, my potential grandchildren. Yawning, she complained about the TV reception, whined because she was an overtired seven-year-old and could not distinguish an object 240,000 miles away. Then she gave into boredom and fell asleep in my lap and missed the actual landing, the human footstep onto this foreign surface. Born into the plastic sixties, she wouldn't tolerate less than perfection.

When I was seven, no astronauts soared above me into the heaven on a journey destined to plant our nation's flag throughout the solar system. Instead, that year Americans by the thousands rushed through dark waters to meet on Normandy Beach, chilled within, invading what had been for many the continent of their origins, my older brother among them. Before he returned home several years later, when the war was over, he penetrated eastward to a concentration camp and saw the fleshless skeletons discarded into mass graves, swallowed the stench of evil deep into his lungs.

And that year I lay in my bed at night, terrified by the airplane noises in the sky, trembling with the hallucination of peering through the ceiling to watch a bomb, fat and dark, drop straight for our house, falling fatter and darker until it exploded with a white flash just above my face. Then I would dive under the blankets and listen for sounds of my mother in the next room, clattering the objects on her nightstand, avoiding the moment when she would have to crawl into her own bed and confront what I now assume must have been night fears about my brother that swarmed over her like vermin.

In that year my father died, a shock, a surprise. We had thought all dangers were reserved for my brother. My father wouldn't go to doctors; he wouldn't take care of himself; he dismissed all pains with a wave of his hand. My memories of him are few. I can't even picture his face. The morning of his death is the impression of him most vivid to me, the noise of groans that woke me from my sleep, the weird slapping of his bare feet as he reeled toward the bathroom, my mother's screams behind him, the hoarse retching of his hemorrhaging, and the final thud of his body as it collapsed onto the tile floor at the base of the sink.

For months afterwards, while my bomb fright dominated me while awake, a nightmare possessed my sleep. My closet door creaking open and a figure hidden amidst the clothes, buried in shadow. Perhaps not a substance, maybe only a pattern of light and darkness. Yet I would lay rigid on my mattress, my heart pounding at the uncertainty. Then the figure would lurch out toward the shaft of moonlight that fell across the room and I would scream myself awake. Even at seven I thought I knew what the dream meant. My father was struggling toward life again, now transformed, a fearful presence of the darkness, and I was desperate to deny him, terrified at the horror he would bring back from death.

Lonely for her son and her husband, my mother occupied herself by talking to me, picking memories of her girlhood from under the scab of time. She spoke of them in a soft voice as if relating a fairy tale, but only basic facts, not revealing the emotion of all that she had endured. Those I've had to conceive of, half inventing a world I've never known.

My mother had been born in Poland, in a village outside Lvov. Years later, by chance, I noticed a book of turn-of-the-century photographs from Poland on the shelf at a friend's apartment. It was a rare book, one of my host's favorite possessions, and he was pleased to spend an hour guiding me through it.

Much of the somber darkness must have been added to by the poor quality of the old cameras, but I suspect it merely accentuated the real gloom that had oppressed the people and the landscape. The buildings were gray, the streets gray, the sky gray, all shades of gray. The country fields looked barren, victims of frost. The people wore black, black hats for the men, black shawls for the women, long black coats and dresses that scraped the dust. The faces were gaunt, hollow with hunger, the dark eyes haunted, only a few decades away from extermination. The eyes seemed to know.

The next morning, I looked up Lvov and my mother's village in a world atlas. They didn't mean a thing to me, just names on a map. For all the stories she had told me, I never could imagine her childhood. It was too foreign; it violated all my assumptions.

Her mother, my unknown grandmother, died when my mother was six, and her father soon remarried a widow with children of her own. I think of that woman as hateful. She made my grandfather abandon his children to accept hers, scatter them among his dead wife's relatives, people who could barely feed themselves.

I imagined my mother and her baby brother ending up with a great aunt, the most impoverished of the lot, a hunched old woman in her eighties who never removed her one black dress, toothless, her scalp covered with sores, smelling of decay. I pictured them living in a hovel, eating a rancid broth, sleeping on piles of filthy rags, kicking away the vermin.

Worst of all, this old woman I conjured had no love in her. She would have been senile; half the time she couldn't remember who the children were, how they had gotten into her cottage.

At the age of seven, my mother had to support herself and her four-year- old brother, each morning making her rounds through the village, knocking on doors, begging to be allowed to do washing or cleaning, the boy tagging after her, clutching her skirt. She knew nothing of money at that age; her payment would come in bread or, if she was lucky, a bowl of stew.

Even now, having read documentation of child labor in mines and factories, I still can't conceive of the seven-year-old girl, my mother, alone in such a grim world, fatigued into stupor by the long day's work, perhaps bitten awake by rats in the darkness.

Eventually, she got to America when she was sixteen. Someone somehow rescued her. She loved this country. Often, she said that she wouldn't be disappointed if she found no heaven after death because she had lived in America and learned that life didn't have to be a horror.

She would have been pleased to witness that flag planted in the surface of the moon, knowing in her heart that life can be much worse than a blurred TV image.

PIN BOY

MINE WAS A CAREER OPTION knocked out from under
me by mid-twentieth-century technology, not the silent
artificial intelligence that threatens many occupations
today, but a clanking contraption of gears, pulleys, and
mechanical grippers that made human hands unneces-
sary.

In my early teens, I had worked several nights a
week as a pin boy in a six-lane bowling alley, a narrow
place that smelled of shellac, spilled beer, and stale tobacco one flight up from our small-town movie theater.
I sat on a ledge in a pit at the end of a gleaming wood
surface, huddling for safety when the bowling balls
came hurtling toward me, my arms and elbows poised
to fend off flying pins, then returning the ball with a
shove down a grooved shaft. After a strike or the second
ball ended the frame with a spare or something like an
8–10 split, I jumped into the pit to press a lever with
my shoe, scoop up scattered pins, and arrange them on
protruding spikes.

That was the pattern of the evening: set them up,
duck for cover, and set them up again. In many ways, it
was a Sisyphean endeavor, but lacking the top of a hill
as an unreachable goal. Pinboying had no such illusion
of an end in sight. Just the ephemeral satisfaction of
seeing the pins neatly aligned before, seconds later, they

were scattered again. A lesson for life. The best laid plans smashed to smithereens.

To be honest, I wasn't cut out for a pin boy future even if technology had not intervened. One lane was all I could handle. As a teenager, I lacked the strength, agility, and stamina of my athletic co-workers, who were able to cover the pin-setting of two adjacent lanes, hopping from one to the other, without the luxury of ducking, constantly pressing and placing and jumping. Amazingly, they were never injured by a flying pin, though we were all in apprehension of those we called Saturday Night Ball Busters—thick, muscled men who heaved balls that sailed above the wood lane until the instant before exploding the pins into lethal projectiles.

I suspect the men who ran the bowling alley, especially Al—the deep-tanned manager always perched on a stool with a cigar and a beer can—were amused by my flailings, their kind words a veiled mockery of my limitations. Every cent I earned as a pin boy, change that never left the cash register, went back to Al to cover the fees of my own bowling and pool table time.

Despite all the hours I devoted to those sports, I never advanced beyond mediocre, in fact, even worse at pool than bowling. At a peach-fuzzed fifteen, as little as I knew about most of life, I was well aware of my mediocrity. Yet I persevered, pushing an immovable rock, desperate to be competent at something, anything.

I have no clear memory of how I became a pin boy, who or what led me up the stairs off to one side of the movie theater where, as a preteen, I had fantasized emulating Roy Rogers' horseback heroism. No memory of when I gripped my first bowling bowl. Or how Al allowed me into the pit. Did I ask? Did he, shorthanded, make an offer?

Pin-setting followed my failures in the food realm, where at our town's vaunted seafood restaurant just down the street from the movie theater, on my initial night as a busboy, I spilled water into a customer's lap the first time I served a table. That led to a rapid transfer into the kitchen and a stool in front of a large bowl of uncooked shrimp. My task was to peel off the shell and scrape out the dark line of innards along the creature's inner curve. With intense concentration, I didn't want to allow a speck to remain. It turned out that my perfectionism made me a very slow shrimp cleaner. The message was delivered calmly and politely, but I was fired that evening, told not to bother coming back the next day.

Even if I had been a champion shrimp deveiner, that skill would have become as useless as pin-setting. Today, shrimp are cleaned by a machine called the Jonsson System. According to the website, "Jonsson machines automatically adjust to each shrimp, gently peeling and deveining it in the style selected. Shrimp are placed in a plastic tray. Briefly, here is how the peeling process works: a clamp grabs a shrimp, the shell is cut and vein removed, pins pull the shrimp from the shell, peeled shrimp are deposited in one location, and the clean shell is then discharged elsewhere." Manual dexterity, fine motor control, would be a wasted excess, assuming I had ever possessed it.

And what about the gross motor control of pin-setting? No humans needed. Now a computerized machine uses a combination of infrared signaling, scanner camera, sweeping bar, automatic scoring system, conveyer belt, ball returner, pin elevator wheel, another conveyer belt, and pin distributor. What does such a machine cost? Ebay offers a used "2 Lane Brunswick Frameworx Bowling Equipment With Glow Anvil Synthetic Lanes" for $18,000.

Assuming such machines had never been invented and human labor remained a necessity, what would I as a hypothetical career pin boy have cost an owner like Al? Assuming ten dollars an hour for a forty-hour week, one year of me (assuming I could have managed two lanes), even forgetting benefits, would have been more than a used machine. Over several years of the machine's life, human labor would have been a serious economic mistake.

My incompetence turned out to be a harbinger. Pin-setting, shrimp-cleaning: They're just two of my failures, authenticated during my early teens, years before the inadequacies of my adulthood. Fortunately, I did manage to stumble upon alternative ways of being. But what if I had had no alternative to life in a pit, ducking and setting through an eternity of frames, my muscles weakening, my bones creaking, my old man's lungs gasping?

HIGH SCHOOL: THE BLEAK YEARS

MY 50TH HIGH SCHOOL REUNION took place in the top room of a pleasure craft that eased out a channel, turned into New York Bay, and sailed under the Verrazano Bridge for a nighttime view of an illuminated Statue of Liberty and a brilliant firework display in the sky over lower Manhattan. We grads wore name tags with photos of our adolescent selves, the only way I could recognize many of them, their one-time shapes lost in expanded middles and multiple chins. But I didn't sense a loss of youth, didn't feel a twinge of A.E. Housman (With rue my heart is laden / For golden friends I had, / For many a rose-lipt maiden / And many a lightfoot lad). Thriving on the golf courses of a happy retirement, spoiling grandchildren, dancing up a storm, my onetime classmates revealed that they had not been stunted by high school.

When I told my friend and colleague Tom Kennedy I was going to the reunion, he suggested that it might be a subject for the Literary Explorer [the series for which this piece was originally written]. My first reaction was to explain to him my high school years had nothing to do with literature. But even as I was typing that email sentence, I realized they did—in a reverse way. That is, if there are such things as matter and anti-matter, there could be literature and anti-literature. My high school experience exemplified the anti-.

In part, the fault lies with me and my classmates, for whom assigned reading intruded upon more imperative adolescent needs. Our class yearbook said of one attractive young woman that she would rather get an F than open a book. But our teachers did nothing but validate that attitude. If their instruction presented what literature was about, we'd rather yawn and carve into the desktops.

Freshman English was devoted to mythology, tales retold in a red-covered text that made the subject more tedious than raking leaves. The high point of the year for me came in the class where I had my manic moment. I had meant to use that text to tap Don Loomas (all names fabricated) on the head in the midst of our whispered dispute over who was a better singer, Vaughn Monroe or Frankie Laine. (Monroe's adenoidal moaning grated on me, a boy who shouted "Mule Train" in the shower.) But the tap landed as a loud thud that silenced the class and even got the attention of our teacher, Mr. Toole. Don reacted by ripping the book from my hand and hurling it out the window.

At the reunion, Don's new wife cornered me to ask if I were really the person responsible for ruining her husband's high school career, the source of the disciplinary troubles that made his parents pull him out of public school for a severe prep school. Don bore no grudges though, was happy to see me, in fact. He thought his parents had overreacted.

We got the impression that Mr. Toole shared our boredom with mythology, would have tossed the text himself, because he preferred to read us his own unpublished short stories about a character named Philip Wedge. The only advantage of the tedious Wedge fictions was that, unlike chapters about the Olympians, they weren't the source of quizzes. Mr. Toole, a wide-hipped man with puffy cheeks and thick, pink-framed glasses, badly wanted to be cool, a role model for the young. He ended up doing that—in a way—when he eloped with a seventeen-year-old senior the year after I graduated. Marcy was rare in our student body because she had intellectual pretensions and must have regarded a teacher who wrote a more appropriate match than boys whose main interests were awkward gropings and dual exhausts. Mr. Toole, of course, lost his teaching job and had to leave town, hauling his trunk of Wedge stories to some new venue.

My sophomore English teacher, a disheveled woman named Miss Welsh, showed up each day with unkempt red hair and the same green tweed suit, the skirt seam always twisted to an unlikely position. Perhaps she had trouble getting up in time to do more than gulp a cup of coffee and throw on the clothes from the day before. Despite her chipper air, she seemed nervous in the classroom, and none of us paid her much attention.

But she was mandated to present *A Tale of Two Cities*, an obligation probably as painful for her as it was for us. Miss Welsh had no more instinct for teaching a novel than she did for combing her hair. We were supposed to have read a chapter for each class, and to make sure we did, she concocted quizzes on the details. What was the color of the teacup Lucie Manette served Sydney Carton? How many stitches did Madame De-Farge knit that evening? I concluded that Dickens was a sadist, deliberately churning out page after page with the sole intention of torturing fifteen-year-olds. I swore never to read a word of his again. That is, until I got to graduate school, discovered *Great Expectations*, and then eagerly enrolled in a Dickens seminar.

Junior-year English is a total blank. I can't remember the teacher or what we were supposed to read. Whatever it was, I didn't do it.

Senior year I was taught by Miss Lydia C. Tern, a woman with a wardrobe of gray dresses and grey hair pulled into a tight bun. The spinster daughter of a clergyman, she had been a school fixture for several generations. Miss Tern took English poetry very seriously, especially the Romantics and Victorians. Deadly serious. I, in contrast, had a much more frivolous attitude toward their works.

With all the wit I could summon in those years, while Miss Tern went on about Tennyson's "Crossing the Bar," I tore out a sheet of notebook paper and used my crude drawing skills to depict a figure stepping across a saloon bar and kicking over beer cans marked XXX.

When I poked the boy next to me and pointed down at my desktop, my artwork evoked a snicker. That piqued curiosity and others craned heads to see what was up. Miss Tern couldn't help but notice. The lesson stopped immediately. The only sounds in the classroom were her footsteps as she approached my desk. She snatched the drawing from under my fingertips, pivoted, and marched back to the front of the room. My drawing stored beneath her grade book, she returned to the beauties of Tennyson—Alfred, Lord.

At the sound of the class-ending bell, she signaled me not to leave. As someone who had been an invisible student for nearly four years, the prospect of punishment was a new experience. I imagined the worst—like what happened when you threw a book out the window. Miss Tern beckoned me to approach her and held the drawing up to my face. "I'm terribly disappointed in you," she said, shaking her head and tsking. "You, a boy whose father has died."

Now, my father died when I was in the third grade, nine years before. So, I wasn't exactly in mourning. Perhaps she expected me to emulate Tennyson's ongoing grief for Arthur Hallam all the years he spent on *In Memoriam*. The best I could do was say sorry, certainly not produce a 131- (plus epilogue) part apology. But my drawing career ended.

It might seem incomprehensible that I would turn to a life of literature after my high school experience. Our house had books, but opening one of them would

have been like conceding to a textbook. Still, as much as
I resented the English assignments of those four years, I
was what I'd call a *closet reader*, choosing paperbacks
from a rack in the local newspaper store with no more
guidance than the cover drawings, usually illustrations
that got a rise from my raging hormones.

Of course, there was Erskine Caldwell's *God's Little
Acre*, which was passed around study halls with the
corners of key pages folded down to shortcut right to
the sex, racy for the standards of the time, but mild stuff
in later days. Slavering over selected passages didn't
count as actually reading a novel, so my schoolmates
maintained their anti-literary integrity.

In contrast, I read from cover to cover, occasionally discovering real literature on that squeaking rack. I
still have the copy of the first Signet paperback printing of *1984* (July, 1950), with a cover drawing of Winston
Smith standing back-to-back with Julia, she in a cleavage-
revealing jump suit, giving him the eye despite her Anti-Sex
League button and the face of Big Brother staring down
at them. The blurb at the top of the cover describes the
novel as "A Startling View of Life in 1984. Forbidden
Love . . . Fear . . . Betrayal."

My reading was closeted—but not because I was
ashamed of the activity, as if it were in itself a betrayal
of some schoolboy vow. Nobody else was reading, none
of my friends. Talk of books would have bewildered
them, a foreign subject wedged into the outgoing di-
alogues about souped-up engines, TV wrestlers, juke-

box hits, and inaccessible girls. Besides, I wouldn't have known what to say, how to express my reactions.

In fact, there was, during my brief science fiction phase, one friend I did speak with. Rob Hill, a robust-looking boy, but homebound and rarely in school because he had hemophilia that required frequent treatments. I visited him now and then to trade sci fi novels and let him draw out my opinions. Bright and upbeat, in spite of his health, Rob had many hours available for reading. That might have been the source of his enthusiasms, his eager conversation, his frequent smiles. As much as his illness cost him, he was spared the dreary routine of the classroom.

By the time I got to college, I had accumulated a small but growing paperback library that became more and more discriminating and more crucial to my identity. Over the years in different apartments and houses, I built sets of shelves, filling entire walls, hauling boxes and boxes every time I moved. Now I've reached advanced years and the stage of jettisoning because there's no more space. During one burst of triage, I gave away twenty-one heavy cartons. Then I put out several hundred books on a shelf along the stairway to my campus office. Happily, almost all found takers, except for a cluster of obscure literary magazines from the 70s. (Does anyone recall the *Falcon* from one of the Pennsylvania state colleges? They rejected my stories several times.)

Also, happily some of my high school classmates

became readers themselves after graduation. When I went to my first reunion, several decades had passed before the planners tracked me down from a list of the lost. It turned out that a number of the group, including the most unlikely, ended up going to college, a few even becoming teachers themselves, a few others travelers to foreign parts.

As I said earlier, I won't put all the blame on our teachers, even Miss Welsh. Maybe we were just reflecting the standard anti-intellectualism of our society. Or maybe it was all the extracurricular traumas of being an adolescent. How could anyone focus on a book with their heads aswirl with raging hormones?

For many decades, I thought it was just me, recalling my high school years as the bleakest of my existence, assuming that the others—the athletes, the drum majorettes, the student council—were having the time of their lives. Then my wife became involved in the planning for her own reunion, surprised to hear the number of in-group people who said, "I was so unhappy in high school."

It would have been cruel to ask for happiness verification on that party boat, interrupt the dancing, the descriptions of trips to the sun, the bragging about successful offspring, the laughter. Today they are happy people.

All of my other literary travels in this series have been to places. The reunion triggered a journey in time. I'm glad I'm not there anymore. It was the life of a stranger.

EXISTENTIALISM AND ABSENT FATHERS

As FAR BACK AS I CAN REMEMBER, in childhood, long before I even knew the word, I was a nascent existentialist. Certainly, I was just lost and alienated, lacking a clear identity, even too confused to realize I was missing one. Many decades later, I have only the vaguest sense of myself as a small boy, an unappealing kid in the few black and white photographs that exist, my expression glum with what must have been incipient angst. Although I played with others, much of the time I was solitary and brooding, alone in my bedroom with a small brown plexiglass Teltone radio, keeping a record of the distant cities that came through after the sun went down. Did I want to be somewhere else? Anywhere? Seeking a place where I belonged?

Only recently did I make the connection between my small boy state of being and the fact that my father had died shortly before my eighth birthday. I had been too young to really grieve, though I do recall a middle of the night darkness when my closet door creaked open and I shrunk with fear that his ghost would emerge. But soon I became inured to being fatherless, much more conscious of just one more difference from other kids than the consequences of his absence. Or so I believed.

A child of middle-aged parents, with a brother and two sisters who were already grown when I was born, I was cared for as part of a truncated family. Still, the oddity of my circumstances—the sense that my existence was an aberration—told me I wasn't a normal kid. Fatherlessness exacerbated it.

Growing up with a father—from what I hear—provides a feeling of continuity, a belonging to some continuum, a fitting in, a place in the larger scheme of things. I wouldn't know. Instead, I wallowed in uncertainties, not knowing who I was, oblivious of any comforts in roots. I was skeptical my identity had more than an accidental connection with family history. Certainly, genetic background provided inclinations and limitations, working ingredients. Height, hair, bad back, paternal bookishness. Yet—essentially—I had to discover and create my identity through involvements with the confusions of the present rather than expecting to rely on being shaped by a past.

Another instinctive, inchoate assumption of my youth finds form in Marcus Aurelius' *Meditations*:

All of us are creatures of a day; the rememberer and the remembered alike. All is ephemeral—both memory and the object of memory. The time is at hand when you will have forgotten everything; and the time is at hand when all will have forgotten you. Always reflect that soon you will be no one, and nowhere.

Decades later, deep in old age, I accept that more than ever.

My father and his father and all the fathers before him—and I—had their days, and they each had to contend with their circumstances to become "myself." Then, aside from a short term of memory from the people who knew them, they became no one, along with their rememberers.

Rather than seize the day, it's grope to find yourself for that day. In effect, I started from scratch to create my own being, unaware of what I was doing for most of my first two decades. Then I discovered Walter Kaufmann's *Existentialism from Dostoevsky To Sartre*, immediately immersing myself in the *Underground Man* and Kierkegaard, Kafka and Lagerkvist, Camus and Sartre, Heidegger and Jaspers—the core of the Existentialists—and realized these were my people.

What I took away primarily was "existence before essence." While I came into the world with genetic traits and inclinations, they didn't constitute an essence. Instead, I was *de trop*, thrown into Being, dangling unmoored, driven to find something to grasp onto. Rather than being born with familial roots, I had to plant my own and seek an agreeable soil for that planting.

Most people don't see it that way. They're content to follow assumed footsteps, fit right into the slots created for them by parental legacy, ethnic heritage, and cultural tradition. Typically, the decisions they make through their lives are constrained by this background, and they are generally content to do so. I wasn't.

The mid-twentieth-century gang of Existentialists lived through the upheavals of World War II. Their footsteps were blasted into dust, all the certainties of their pre-war lives demolished. Their decisions were made *in extremis*, in the shadow of a firing squad or death camp. Daily life had become a fateful trial. No way could they rely on the past. They had to create and recreate themselves again and again, often with each decision they made.

I realize that for everyone else the death of a father hardly compares with a world in upheaval, mass murder and destruction all around. That war was taking place during my childhood, at its height the month my father died. My only involvement was toy soldiers and a brother off in the uncertainties of European combat. Family anxiety underlay the daily doings in my house.

Still, in addition to war, an absent father appears to have a role in the making of an Existentialist. Camus never knew his, the man—Lucien—killed in World War I when Albert was less than a year old. Sartre's died when Jean-Paul was an infant, a happening the son welcomed, according to his autobiography, *Words*:

> There is no good father, that's the rule. Don't lay the blame on men but on the bond of paternity, which is rotten. To beget children, nothing better; to *have* them, what iniquity! Had my father lived, he would have lain on me at full length and would have crushed me.

True to his words, Sartre never had children, nor did fellow Existentialists de Beauvoir, Nietzsche, and Kierkegaard. Maurice Merleau-Ponty was five when his officer father was killed in World War I. He remained close to his mother and claimed to have a happy childhood. Unlike the other Existentialists who came from a bourgeois background, he did not rebel against that life style, often to the annoyance of the others. Seemingly content, his theory of the central role of bodily perception of a provisional, open-ended world meant that our selves are in a perpetual state of becoming.

Sartre described him as a man "hopelessly pining for his childhood" and as a philosopher driven by wonder like a "child scandalized by our futile grown-up certitudes, who asks shocking questions which the adults never answer."

But a father doesn't have to be dead to be absent. The vacancy can be a deep force even if the man is sitting in a chair on the other side of the room, a physical presence, an emotional dearth.

I suppose I'm fortunate that my father was not a domineering bully and did not commit suicide, from all accounts a decent man who merely died quickly one morning from a sudden aneurism. I never knew enough about him to reject him. Instead, these writers who lacked a sense of their own fathers or who rebelled against the fathers they knew came to serve as my intellectual fathers—as much as they disagreed with each other and as much as I disagreed with them on specific ideas. They offered me an explanation for my own grappling with the world as I strove to create an ongoing identify, the alternative of an essence.

Simone de Beauvoir, Merleau-Ponty's Sorbonne classmate, was far more representative than he of the Existential group in excoriating her origins, most directly in the sarcastic *Memoirs of a Dutiful Daughter*, where she describes her alienation from her father, who encouraged her intellectual development but ended up complaining that he had "created a monster" when she surpassed him. The combative situation of her family led to the feminist protest of *The Second Sex*.

She wasn't the only father obsessive. A present, living father served as a fundamental dilemma for others considered proto-Existentialists. Kafka's tyrannical father, hardly a role model, appears to be the source of oppressive, humiliating forces endured by the characters in fictions. Søren Kierkegaard was haunted by his depressive, guilt-ridden father, again and again exploring the themes of sacrificial father/son relationships, of inherited sin, of the burden of history, and of the centrality of the "individual, human existence relationship, the old text, well known, handed down from the fathers."

Fyodor Dostoevsky's father, Mikhail, cruel, volatile, sullen, and alcoholic, made his family home cold and austere. His son could never depict a happy childhood in his writings. In *The Brothers Karamazov*, the degenerate and heartless father is killed by his assumed-illegitimate son, the malevolent Smerdyakov. Fyodor getting revenge through written words.

Friederich Nietzsche did lose his father as a child. Carl, a Lutheran minister, died when Nietzsche was four or five—younger than I was—leading to a long mourning and, according to some biographers, the reason for his famous "God is dead," Nietzsche abandoning his heritage and blaming the deity for taking away his father. The death of his father meant the death of the deity.

In Ernest Hemingway's writings existentialist rootlessness prevails. His physician father committed suicide when his son was thirty. Although Ernest emulated that father with his own death—one of several suicides in the Hemingway family, the characters of his fiction lacked pasts, displaced from the places of their origins, struggling for self-creation.

Edmund Husserl and Gabriel Marceau, while having fathers long into their adulthood, engaged in a form of religious rebellion—Husserl abandoning Judaism to become a Lutheran soon after the death of his father, Marceau rejecting his father's agnosticism and converting to Roman Catholicism while the parent was still alive. Simone Weil, herself dying only in her thirties, a child of Jewish parents, found a deep faith in Christ and became a Christian ascetic, buried in a Catholic cemetery.

All of these writers and thinkers abandoned the worlds they had been born into and, with often extreme struggle, formed their own beliefs, their own understandings of what human life was all about; in effect, creating themselves.

I'll admit to not knowing much about other people—what goes on inside their heads when they're not absorbed in the minutiae of the quotidian, what they think about when watching TV or driving to work or waking in 3 a.m. darkness. How do they feel about the jobs they do, about their families, about their finances, about their futures? Was Thoreau right? Do the mass of men—and women—lead lives of quiet desperation? Or was that in a time of widespread deprivation? Does a flat screen TV make life less desperate? Few, I'm sure, would be content to admit that they are creatures of a day, their existence an ephemeral wisp.

Once people reach adulthood, they find themselves having to fill a succession of days, devoting much of the time to some job that enables them to support themselves. In fact, work is a fundamental time filler for most, and not just the hours on the job, but also those thinking and talking about it and worrying about it. People tend to find a self-identity in their occupations.

Yet, I can't help remembering the waiter in Sartre's *Being and Nothingness* used to exemplify *mauvaise foi*—bad faith. As he serves table after table, ingratiating himself with diners, he's merely playing a role, inauthentic. But does he know he's pretending, behaving according to an inherent script that he allows to be imposed upon him? And when he's not at his restaurant job, say, as husband, father, son, friend? Is he still displaying a contrived identity, enacting learned patterns, replicating the behavior of his father, fulfilling external expectations?

Without a father to emulate—the usual path of this is the way things are done—I sought alternative guidelines to know how to be. My problem was that I knew it, recalling a time as a college freshman when I admitted to myself, "I'm really out of it," but without any idea of how to get "with it." And so, I received a degree, married, and took an assumed-desirable job as an executive trainee, a career route that guaranteed a future of good suits and cushy perks.

Two months into that position—about the same time I discovered Camus' *The Myth of Sisyphus*—I wanted out. By then I had gained a very clear sense of the years ahead, the progression of job titles and better offices, bigger cars and houses, and the mundane duties that were little more than make-work. Although I hadn't yet read *Being and Nothingness*, I knew instinctively that I would be a version of Sartre's waiter in the bad faith of my executive performance.

Paradoxically, while the original Existentialists experienced their self-discovery though involvement in a cataclysmic war, I was fortunate to enjoy the options of a flexible peacetime to make my decisions. Having a choice was an accidental luxury of the time—despite years of on-the-edge finances and deeper miseries. At another time, in other circumstances, I probably would have floundered in unhappiness, self-punishing my bad faith.

In the process of forming myself, I regret a number of foolish choices and misguided actions. Certainly, the Existentialists were hardly paragons. Despite their courage and insight, much that they did in their private lives was stupid, shameful, and—even to their admirers—embarrassing.

Self-creation doesn't guarantee happiness or fulfillment. In fact, the heightened awareness may make it impossible to hide from failures and inadequacies. But bad faith no longer provides a refuge. Existence is just one decision after another, the notion of a stable essence a pipedream. We keep pushing that rock, never reaching the goal. Camus concludes *The Myth of Sisyphus* with the apparently optimistic, "We must imagine Sisyphus happy." Hemingway might respond with, "Isn't it pretty to think so."

What would my long-absent father think of me, given the illusion that he was looking down from some sort of continuum? Would it matter? He was just a creature of the day, vanished into Nothingness. The clock is still ticking on my day. Then, poof. Oblivion, like my dad. All those excruciating choices ultimately meaningless.

WINNING IS EVERYTHING: HOW I SOLD OUT

WHEN I WAS AN UNDERGRADUATE at Rutgers, our varsity football team lost many more games than it won. But we went anyway, wearing tweed sports jackets, our dates in plaid skirts, corsages pinned to their blazers, containers of orange blossom—gin and orange juice— hidden in the folds of a stadium blanket. Most of the time we ignored what was happening on the field, occasionally diverted by action that roused half-ironic cheers, chanting a school song after our infrequent touchdowns. We had few illusions about victory. Our pleasure came in being part of a playful crowd on a fall afternoon.

My freshman year, to earn a few needed dollars, I showed up early the Sunday morning after a home game to work on the cleaning crew, wearing gloves, walking up and down the now empty stadium rows, stooping to pick up cups and wrappers and crumpled game programs, dragging a bag of litter after me, then dumping it into a larger container, and returning to the next row. No cheers. No joys. The aftermath.

I had no way of realizing that experience was a harbinger for the future of college football: loud noise, a few thrills, and a mess to sweep up. Wasted millions, torn joints, concussed brains, phony grades.

In those days I was still a sports fan, at the tail end of a thrall from boyhood when my mother let me subscribe to *The Sporting News*, and I read every page's picayune details down to the reports on class D minor league baseball. I rooted for the St. Louis Cardinals and to this day can still reel off the starting lineup of the 1946 World Series winning team, include the starting pitchers. Evenings I listened to hockey games on the tiny Teletone radio at my bedside. Boxing matches too, not realizing the fever pitch of the announcer's voices had little to do with the two men stalking each other around a ring and throwing occasional punches.

Lacking the coordination for any athletic ability, in high school I served as scorekeeper for basketball games and worked as a stringer calling in reports of football games to several local papers, a step in my goal of becoming a sportswriter.

My freshman year at Rutgers, I joined the sports staff of the campus paper, *The Targum*, and was assigned to cover the cross-country track team, wandering out to a field and watching guys running in what seemed aimless circles. It was boring. But reporting on football was the privilege of juniors and seniors.

My fraternity brother Paul was a starting end for a couple of seasons, managing to fit in practice and travel to away games while mastering the demands of mechanical engineering and waiting lunch tables with me to work off part of our board. No coaches or rabid alums slipped him envelopes thick with cash or the keys to a new car. Paul, like his teammates, just enjoyed the sport, one more satisfied athlete in a long historical heritage at the university.

Rutgers enjoys the distinction of being the college where the first intercollegiate football game took place on November 6, 1869. The rules were a mix of soccer and rugby, with no passing or carrying, basically just kicking. Rutgers defeated Princeton 6 to 4, one of a handful of times Rutgers defeated their nearby rivals over the next century plus. The competition ended in 1980 when Rutgers decided to go big-time and lost its way.

I've been thinking of Paul recently (the 2019 season) when Rutgers football team—despite the millions spent over the years on scholarships, an expanded stadium, training facilities, and million-dollar coaches—was humiliated by Iowa 30 to 0. I had spent five years at the University of Iowa, one more than I did at Rutgers, and many Iowa football players had been my friends and students.

Rutgers enjoys the distinction of being the American university that's wasted the most money on a dream football, with little to show for it. Each dismal football year seems a source of deep shame for Rutgers, its alumni, its students, and the entire state of New Jersey. How could Rutgers have the nerve to call itself a first-class university with its team regularly humiliated?

Over the years, the university's presidents have pledged commitment to a successful football program.

Politicians fussed. Alumni fumed. Much was at stake. Reputations. Careers. Budgets.

We live in a country that craves sports stars and winning teams. Despite the substance abuse, assaults, rapes, and gun crimes committed by athletes, many cases never get to court, and penalties are slight, at least for current players. Athletes live according to different rules, and college administrators dare not challenge the system, and in many cases, they don't want to. Coverup of athletes' crimes and scandals is one of our national dirty little secrets. Actually, even when exposed, it elicits a few perfunctory editorials, but mainly shrugs. In many cases, students, alumni, and even politicians blame the whistleblowers for damaging the prospects of the team. It's happened at Rutgers too. Winning is everything.

The sad news from my undergraduate alma mater reminded me of my involvements with big-time college sports and my complicity in a sellout of academic standards. Now reformed, I have a need to confess my transgression, get it off my chest. It happened when I was a graduate student at Iowa, teaching basic literature sections. In the unlikely possibility of repercussions for long-ago events, I won't use real names of the people involved, except that of a then well-known basketball player.

I knew about the sports obsessions of Big Ten schools even before I arrived and lived in a tin hut just a short walk from the football stadium. But I soon realized how extreme those obsessions were. Only a limited number of seats far from the fifty-yard line were available to students, who had to line up for more than an hour in the middle of the week to claim one before the game. And it wasn't just alumni who got the good seats. The university's team seemed to represent the hopes and pride of the entire state, wealthy farmers flying their personal Cessnas to the local airfield on Saturday mornings, the not-so-affluent driving hundreds of miles. At Rutgers Stadium in my day half the seats were empty, and students had ideal perspectives for those occasional moments we followed the action on the field.

My second indication of football's dead seriousness for Iowans came a few weeks into my first semester there. Late in that season, the team had been ranked number one in the nation, bound for the Rose Bowl, only one final game with Minnesota remaining. But Minnesota won by just a field goal, 10 to 7, if memory serves. No number one, no Rose Bowl. And at the beginning of my freshman writing class the following Monday, one of the young women was in tears. "It was mean of them to beat us like that," she lamented.

Eventually, I came to know a number of the players, mainly the recruited African Americans who drank the same watery 3.2 percent beer at the same bar as we did. These were big, muscular men, coddled by recruiters and coaching staff, some touted as potential all-Americans. At their parties I first heard Ray Charles records and at their picnics tasted world-class barbecued ribs.

For most, the *raison d'etre* for being at the university was football, packing on training table pounds and practicing hours on end for the glory of a trip to a major bowl, the dream of an NFL career. A fullback I'll call Bob explained the players' lives. Both of us from New Jersey, we connected for a dinner together. Bob had been a star athlete and tops in his class at a large Jersey City high school, one of the many local players Rutgers failed to recruit. At Iowa he majored in Russian and went on to earn a law degree, followed by a successful career as an attorney. But as bright and committed a student as he was, he told me how difficult it was to focus on education, what with the exhausting training schedule and the temptations of under-the-table cash payments, gift automobiles, and willing women.

Bob was atypical in his academic background. Many, if not most, of the others I knew had been plucked from poverty and deficient inner-city high schools in cities like Detroit or Chicago, dropped into the midst of cornfields, hog farms, and innocent blond-haired, blue-eyed youth. Most ended up in majors like physical education or recreation on the advice of assistant coaches, some of whom taught the courses in those programs.

Clarence, a small, slight African American man who came to the parties, a non-athlete who had chosen to major in recreation out of genuine interest, told me about a course he was taking. On the first day the instructor announced his grading system: football players would get As, his friends Bs, and everyone else Cs. My friend raised his hand and asked, "I'm not a football player. Am I your friend?" Clarence got a C.

Somehow, a number of athletes gravitated to my core literature classes, probably because they heard I knew other players and figured a friend of a friend would treat them well. With one exception, I don't recall doing anyone special favors beyond advice on revising papers. They earned whatever grades they got. Now and then coaches sent forms to check on progress, but no pressure.

Not for me, at least. But I did have a friend teaching freshman writing who had been born in Korea, at that time only in the U.S. for a few years. In the middle of a party in my tin hut, this man I'll call Lee announced, "I am very annoyed that the basketball coach keeps calling me about a student in my class named Cornelius Hawkins." That stopped everyone cold, bottles about to be poured, potato chips about to be bitten, hands in suspended animation, until someone spoke. "That's Connie Hawkins, Lee. He's a great basketball player."

And he was, recruited from New York City, perhaps the most sought after high school star in the country that year, landed by Iowa. In those days, freshmen were not allowed to play varsity sports. Hawkins was limited to halftime demonstrations, awing the crowds with his skills, shooting two balls at once and sinking both. At this time in Iowa basketball history Don Nelson, an all-American and future NBA coaching legend, had another year of eligibility left. Mouths watered at the prospect of a team that featured both Nelson and Hawkins.

That's why someone urged, "Lee, you've got to pass him." According to those who claimed to know, Hawkins's performance on the American College Test was as abysmal as his performance on the basketball court was sensational. Others agreed that he must not fail. Lee relented. "If he comes to class and turns in his assignments, he will get at least a D." The partygoers sighed. A crisis averted.

It turned out that Lee's promise didn't matter. Hawkins was implicated in a gambling scandal, something about shaving points in high school games so scores wouldn't make the spread. He dropped out of Iowa and lost an opportunity for an NBA career. By the time he was cleared of the accusations, he had passed his ideal playing age, limited to a few mediocre years in the now defunct American Basketball Association.

We—those of us at the party—had conspired to abandon academic integrity and inveigle an innocent immigrant in the plot. It was a disgraceful act. But Nelson and Hawkins on the same team. Think of it.

My one actual collusion in giving special preference to an athlete was of a different nature. It wasn't to improve a team or thrill spectators. It was to help a friend we believed had been screwed by the system. Several of us cooperated to bring up his grade point average and get him off probation.

Here's what happened. The man I'll call Chaz was

yet another New Jersey high school star who didn't choose Rutgers. He was a lineman, a guard. That was before I got to know him, before he was involved in an accident, driving a car that crossed a railroad track and somehow encountered a train. An Iowa coed was with him. Her presence may have been a factor in the way the athletic program dropped him. They both survived, but Chaz's back was permanently injured, at least to the extent that it would have been dangerous for him to play football again, not with his inflexible walk. Halfway to a degree, but with a deficient GPA, he lost his athletic scholarship. Still he was determined to finish his BA, borrowing money for out-of-state tuition. He married, and his wife—a sweet and lovely woman—moved out from New Jersey. They were a fine couple and we liked them both very much, pleased when they showed up at parties.

So, we formed a plan to help Chaz, rationalizing our conspiracy with outrage that the university would cut off an injured player whose grades suffered because the pressure to practice forced him to give short shrift to his studies. A number of us, including several who went on to distinguished prize-winning careers in American letters, worked closely with Chaz, enrolled him in their classes, tutored and edited, to assure that he would receive no grade less than a B. And that's what I gave him in my course. Chaz got off probation and graduated. I still think it was the right thing to do.

But I did no more favors for functioning athletes.

In my last semester at Iowa, a compact running back I knew casually and will call Clyde had registered for my core lit class, his name printed on the official roster. He never attended class, not once. When it came time to turn in a grade, I asked the director of the core lit program for advice. You have to fail him, he told me. It was the rule.

Then one day that summer, living in New Jersey again, ready to start a career at another university, I heard my phone ring. It was Clyde. He explained he thought he had used up his playing eligibility and, so, saw no sense in going to classes. But he had just learned he actually had another year left. Could we work out some way for him to make up the F. Nothing, I told him. It was too late.

I don't believe Clyde ever made the pros. Not because of the lost year. He just wasn't big enough, probably not good enough. But colleges shouldn't provide farm teams for the pros, shouldn't exploit players with that low-percentage dream to fatten the athletic budget and cater to fans. They shouldn't concoct phony grades to assure eligibility. The rest of us shouldn't involve our egos in the success of our school's or our state's teams, as if their victories enhanced our self-worth. Not at the price of integrity.

I recall going to Bakers Field in New York to watch a Rutgers-Columbia game on a day of a chill, heavy rain. I watched my table-waiting partner, Paul, running though the downpour, being tackled in the mud, ending up filthy and soggy. I asked him about it the next day. Rutgers lost, but he told me he had had the time of his life. That was back in the days when college football actually had something to do with sports.

My Last Panty Raid

FULLY AWARE THAT I'M OPENING MYSELF up to a barrage of abuse in the Twittersphere, I'm still willing to admit that I was present at a panty raid on a college campus. It took place many years ago, on an early April day in 1957 after a foot of snow led to the official cancellation of classes and a feeling that we had suddenly fallen into in an alternative reality where all rules swirled in limbo. The spirit of carnival reigned, though we weren't in masks and costumes—just warm coats and thick gloves.

Though it may seem a lame excuse, I just stood on the sidelines, observing while dozens of male students charged into a women's dormitory. The whole event was totally unexpected, unplanned, spur of the moment. For me, at the time, the raid was much less an example of sexist behavior than an illustration of the madness of crowds.

Here's what happened. It was the final months of my senior year at Rutgers College when I woke up to look out my fraternity house window and saw nothing but white all around me, not a car on the street, and barely a person. I was scheduled for a test in the music building that morning, and—though I knew it was foolhardy—put on boots and began my trek through virgin snow, mine the only visible footsteps, a deep trailblazing. The door to the music building was locked, no sign posted. I grabbed the handle and tugged a few times, just in case.

By the time I walked back to my frat house, other students were out, stomping new paths, calling greetings of disbelief to one another, relishing in the unexpected free day, the rarity of an April snow. The sky was clear after the all-night dumping, the temperature still cold. The white around us gleamed, thick on the roofs and tree limbs.

The frolicking students were all male because in those days Rutgers was a men's college, women students a few miles away on the other side of New Brunswick at Douglass College. We considered ourselves fortunately in the proximity. Princeton men had to travel long distances across state lines to schools like Wellesley and Mt. Holyoke just for a date.

The Rutgers-Douglass arrangement plays a central role in the events of that evening. I don't recall the next hours of daylight. We probably hung out in the fraternity, some playing bridge, some listening to music, some even reading. Shortly after dinner, the house's one pay phone rang. Whoever answered made the announcement. It was the women in Douglass's Jameson C dorm building challenging us to a snowball fight. The Jameson Hall complex was a three-story brick complex divided into separate units. Considering the number of women in C and the number of men in our fraternity, it would mean a pretty much even match.

But when the sun went down and a group of us stepped out into the fraternity row of Union Street, we found ourselves swallowed into a mass of several hundred males all headed toward Douglass and the Jameson campus. An out-of-step march through the streets of the town, much chatter and laughter, hands dipping into snow, a few balls thrown in feigned practice for the real battle.

When we arrived on Jameson, more men joined our group from another directions. We milled about, no women in sight. I did spot one former freshman roommate deep in the crowd. Lou had flunked out at his first try at being a student, enlisted in the army, and now was back. His flunking had been no surprise. He had spent most of his time cooing seductive phone calls into the dorm's hallway payphone, hanging out in bars when he wasn't with a woman, and stealing souvenirs. Our room had a bar stool from Princeton's Nassau Inn as his desk chair, a metal highway marker from the former New Jersey route 69 (now 31, a change from the suggestive number I attribute to Lou's thefts), and a six-foot wide red sign that said "Rabbits for Sale" hung across a wall. One Tuesday afternoon when I was alone reading an assignment, a state trooper came to the room and collected all of Lou's plunder. As far as I know, he was never arrested. But he did fail every exam. And here he was, back again, though not the instigator that evening. We waved to each other.

For a time, we all milled around, waiting for something to happen. Men were shouting at the women peering out the dorm windows. "Come out and fight!" "Don't be sissies!" But the women knew they were far outnumbered, a handful against hundreds. Yet some goaded back, calling jeers like, "Come and get us." That was a mistake.

A worse mistake was the act of one young woman who unlocked a door to crack it open a bit for more taunting. In an instant, several men heaved their bodies to push it wide. But from where I was positioned in the midst of the crowd, I could see that they stood frozen in the entranceway, not sure what to do next. We had all come for a snowball fight, and that wasn't happening. Would those at the door drag the women out?

Then someone, just one voice in the crowd—I never learned whose—yelled, "Panty raid!" The melee began, men storming through the door, women screaming— mock screams for the most part. It couldn't have been all of the men. There wasn't nearly enough room. Perhaps they entered in shifts, whooping and shouting, emerging back into the night bras, panties, girdles, and stockings held high. Trophies. Spoils of the battle.

I never thought to go into that dorm, more interested in watching the behavior of the others, nonplussed by the sudden turn. Besides, I was engaged, just a few months from being married. What did I want with a stranger's unmentionables? Even if the evening had fulfilled the intended snowball fight, I doubt that I would have thrown more than a few, content to observe the action on the white lawn, write about it for the campus paper.

Eventually, the male raiders dwindled to a handful, perhaps because there were no undergarments left, perhaps because it had all become redundant. Finally, the women were able to lock their door and the men to wander back across town. So that was a panty raid, everyone must have been thinking.

Actually, ours took place late in the history of the phenomenon, a national undergraduate prank that began in 1949 and reached its peak in the early fifties. It was considered just something students did—like squeezing into phone booths or having food fights and pep rallies. By all accounts, the last of the raids took place in the early sixties. By that time, in the wake of the costs of property damage, some students were being expelled. That put a damper on things. Our own panty raid was a one-time adventure, the first and the last all in one.

The next day, roads plowed, paths cleared, classes were held as usual. The Dean of Men summoned all of the fraternity chapter presidents to his office, droning with his usual stone face. He told us we should be ashamed. A blot on the reputation of Rutgers. One statement I still remember to this day: "Some of those women have lost some very expensive undergarments." The rebuke ended with each fraternity obligated to collect what its members had scavenged.

Our house had a plain brown cardboard box in the front hallway near the mail basket. Slowly, it began to fill up with silk and nylon and cotton, dropped off men's fingertips. I expected laughter, comments, horseplay. Instead, the gathering was mainly done in silence, one person at a time, members—I surmised—more embarrassed by what they had done than concerned about the women's financial burden.

The boxes from each fraternity were taken to the dean's office, stacked in awkward layers. I remember wondering how any garment would get back to its owner and, more so, whether that owner would be willing to wear it after all the hands it had been through. Much like trampled snow.

I wonder if back then the women in the dorm had felt violated, if those who remember that night do now even if they hadn't then. A few probably did and still do. Throughout history, groups of men have done much worse to women in their manic rages. The panty raid, all things considered, was one more example of a college fad of the time. Still, it illustrates the madness of crowds and potential for damage to more than a few flimsy garments.

Real damage.

IRRESPONSIBLE AND MALADJUSTED

"IRRESPONSIBLE" AND "MALADJUSTED." Those are the exact words the then-Governor of New Jersey, Robert B. Meyner, applied to me. Actually, his full statement about an editorial I had published in our student newspaper was, "an irresponsible article by a maladjusted boy."

Today, the request I made would be considered quaint, more laughable than irresponsible. But I suppose I still could be seen as having aged into a maladjusted octogenarian. Proving that while times change, people don't.

The source of this headline-producing social-political outrage in the mid 1950s was my brief editorial in the then-four-day-a-week Rutgers *Targum*, where I had a title as one of several senior editors. My plea was essentially, "Let the Girls into the Dormitories." And all I was asking for were a few hours of visiting times, not steamy overnights. Rutgers was at the time a men's college, women removed three miles across town at Douglas College.

Today I probably would raise much more outrage for calling young women in college "girls" than I would for opening doors of sexual license. But remember that the governor called me a "boy." Perhaps behind this nomenclature was the fact that, for many, I was threatening the assumption of childhood innocence, the parental notion that their Jimmy and Susie shouldn't be tempted to sully their purity.

I'm reminded of a duty assigned to me several years before the editorial when I was a fraternity pledge: Go to one of the living cottages across town on a Douglass campus and survey how many of the young female residents were virgins. "We all are," insisted the two who answered the door. Did the young women have their fingers crossed? They certainly had been more amused than outraged, faint smiles on their faces.

While, in those days, males could roam about day and night, women were protected by curfews, as I recall 8 p.m. weeknights for freshmen and midnight for all on weekends. My own fraternity house had a dimly lit make-out room when the Saturday night action was hot and heavy until about 11:30. Cinderella's dilemma was an archetype. Hairdos restored, skirts untwisted.

While I couldn't provide a statistical breakdown, I knew anecdotally at the time that virginity appeared to be more exception than reality. While women's residences had curfews, the frequent ruse was signing out for a weekend at home where parents, if they even expected their daughters, were more lenient than housemothers.

My coed visitation plea was not frivolous, not a wink and a nod to insatiability. That was a time when people married early, men often immediately after college graduation, their new wives, most often an academic two or three years behind, dropping out for the wedding ring. People were, in fact, making major life decisions. I argued in my piece that they needed an opportunity for serious conversations, to really learn about each other, in a way that wasn't possible while groping in a make-out room or parked car with a curfew looming. I also had the advantage of conversational time, dating and eventually being engaged to a young woman attending another college and living at home. Why not those confined to campus?

Of course, I didn't make my case very effectively, my words more blurted than reasoned. I also made the blunder of writing, "We're not celibate," misusing the term because I was unaware of its religious overtones. Not only did I offend Governor Meyner, the Trenton diocese of the Roman Catholic Church spewed fire and brimstone as if the ninth circle of Dante's hell would be too light a punishment.

In what appears to have been a significant backstory, my ill-put few hundred words became a live grenade in a battle over which university would house a new medical school in a state that, up till then, lacked one. Seton Hall University, a Catholic institution, eventually got it. I apparently was instrumental in making the case that secular Rutgers failed the moral test of caring for the health of millions. If the university had been lax enough to admit people like me as an undergraduate, what even more shameful misdeeds lay ahead?

Beyond condemnation by Church and State, I became an overall cause célèbre. Newspapers wrote about controversial me, often tongue-in-cheek. Coincidentally, college senior men in general had been receiving flyers for a sexual manual, which led the *Daily Princetonian* to suggest that those at Rutgers were far past the need for such instruction.

On my own campus, I was summoned before a group of students and administrators called the Targum Council for possible censure, the Dean of Men chairing the meeting. I had written a much longer explanation of the reasoning behind my editorial in advance. The paper's editor-in-chief suggested that I be allowed to read it. "That's even worse than the original," some people said, their faces distressed. But the editor, my friend Doc, argued that if they censured me, he would have to allow me to defend myself by printing my explanation. That struck me as a good idea, and so, when the censure motion came up for vote, I was the only one who raised my hand Yes.

The Council members, and certainly the Dean, had been unaware that my defending editor, who had been out of town at a convention of college newspaper editors the day I wrote my piece, ending up in a one-night-stand with a woman who went on to become a TV journalist. It happened in a hotel, not a dormitory or frat house. His being the playing cat away while I was the inhibited mouse probably had something to do with his stand at the meeting.

Still, I was a bit of a persona non grata on campus. One event that stands out was my suppression at a student assembly in which members of a senior honor society called "Cap and Skull" tapped the next year's inductees and made brief presentations. There were twelve of us, I had been selected in the spring the year before my editorial. This time I was seated in the back, leper-like, silenced, stepping forward only when my turn to tap a successor—literally placing a cap on his head—then quickly hustled back to insignificance.

Considering my infamy, I did worry about getting employment after graduation, especially because I had marriage plans. That was before fast food and flipping burgers. But would a menial equivalent be my life ahead? Instead, I ended up with a plum position, an internship with General Electric, which it turned out led to a career I didn't want,when I should have chosen a life of teaching and writing, where being maladjusted allowed me to fit right in.

All this was more than a half century ago, and since then ironies have abounded.

Once gaining the medical school, Seton Hall found its operation a budget-buster, ceding the operation to the state as part of a New Jersey College of Medicine and Dentistry. That institution was, several years ago, merged with Rutgers University as Rutgers' Medical College. Recently, Seton Hall opened another medical school with Hackensack Meridian Hospital, which may have a more substantial financial base, though I hear rumors.

And what about women in dormitories? The flood-gates opened years ago, restraints swept away with any notion of curfews. Dorms became coed, visitations and overnights abounding. Remember the sexual revolution? I recall being at a lunch table where the woman in charge of student activities at the university where I teach shook her head as she told us how senior men were complaining about the predatory freshmen women hitting on them. I suspect my pledge avatar would have gotten a very different response to the survey question about virginity. Would he have gotten out of the room with his own intact?

It wasn't just coed dorms. Birth control pills and legal abortion were probably even more vital forces of social change, making dorm cohabitation much less fraught with fears of pregnancy. Several friends of my undergraduate years ended up in early marriages, as seniors moving from a fraternity house to an apartment large enough for wife and newborn. Marriages of that period lasted, at least from the evidence of my generational cohort. Is the reason love or inertia?

From what I've read lately, sex as well as marriage is a diminishing activity for twenty-first century young people, a significant percentage not even bothering to date, much less cohabitate. If they did end up in the same dorm room, would they just stare at separate screens and tweet? Would a survey of virginity result in open-mouthed confusion?

I may be a sentimental old fool, but—in memory—the sexual tensions of my youth were animating and energizing. Anticipation and frustration. It certainly gave us much to talk about openly and fantasize about privately. Consider all those movies, stories, novels, and songs that would never have been created without the lure of sexual potential. Birds do it, bees do it, even college students with curfews want to do it. And many actually did. Let's be irresponsible—despite deans and governors.

THE MILITARY-INDUSTRIAL COMPLEX AND ME

FRESH OUT OF COLLEGE, I became a functionary in the military-industrial complex. Dwight David Eisenhower was still President and had not yet given a name to the behemoth, much less warning the nation of its predatory powers. Besides, what did I know? I was twenty-one and needed a job, a career, something to sustain me in the life ahead. General Electric offered a future in Advertising and Sales Promotion. And so, with no work experience beyond summers as a bus boy and after-class hours as a bookstore clerk, I found myself in a cubicle eight hours a day editing ships' turbine instruction manuals and playing surreptitious games of hang-the-man with my coworkers to break the tedium. This was suit-and-tie real life, my first trainee assignment. In another forty-some years I could retire.

The bête noir of our working lives was someone I'll call Mr. Wardlaw, the Navy inspector of manuals, a civilian, a dry man with pale skin, thin hair, rimless glasses, and a croaked voice, who tssked over misplaced commas and denied approval of a manual at the whiff of a typo. At a later time, one might have called him computerized, except that computers occasionally crash. Mr. Wardlaw droned along with flawless consistency, exemplifying an ideal of military precision, more likely to sell secrets to the enemy than crack a smile.

His office was located far back in the manufacturing area, a long walk from my cubicle, where men with real skills spent their days engulfed by great whirrings and poundings as they constructed huge turbines that someday, if Mr. Wardlaw approved the instructions, would actually propel a ship. How such a ship would function never occurred to me. My work life was all pencil and paper, disengaged from the world's vast oceans. Hang-the-man and a brownbag lunch were the high points of my days.

That was the routine. Hours of assuring the figure number on each drawing matched the number in the text, checking that every margin was aligned, and then a monthly visit to Mr. Wardlaw, manual in hand like a supplicant before the king. Then, one morning my manager—Weldon Dick, let's name him—called me into the chair facing his barren desk. He was a squat man, mustache scrunched over a perpetual cigar, legendary in our cubicle for returning to work duties an hour after his first child was born. Foul smoke hung heavy between us. I choked back a coughing fit.

"The economy is not good this year," he muttered to break the ice. I nodded, knowing as little about the economy as I did about turbines. "Our department needs new business." He paused, and I nodded again. New business seemed reasonable. "The Missile and Space Vehicle Division has offered us the opportunity to produce proposals to the military for new weapons systems."

Finally, I spoke. "Good."

"We need someone to go to Philadelphia to coordinate the project."

This time I didn't even nod. Why was he telling me about it?

"We want you to go."

Me? What did I know about proposals? About Philadelphia? Where would I live? Totally ignorant of expense accounts, I even assumed I would have to pay for my lodgings in that city as well as my apartment in Schenectady. "Mr. Dick," I said. "If you're considering anyone else for the assignment, let him win."

Dick removed the cigar from his mouth, cleared his throat, and looked at the ceiling. "We've already had to let some people go this year. Without new business, there may be others." Even I caught on. A few days later, I boarded a train to Philadelphia to turn out proposals for weapons systems.

Today I'd barely trust anyone like the kid I was then to change my oil. But there I was. Hang-the-man and Mr. Wardlaw one day, responsible for bidding on a $300-million project the next.

I did catch on to expense accounts very quickly. A secretary, Barbara, in our case, actually delivered into my hands plane tickets and cash advances. I liked going up to her and saying, "Barbara, I need four hundred dollars," and stuffing the bills in my wallet an hour later. I liked telling desk clerks who claimed no available accommodations, "I'm with GE," and having a room suddenly materialize.

I was, however, much less confident about being able to produce a proposal by the deadline. Deadlines, Weldon Dick emphasized many times in the hours before I left Schenectady, were something the military took very seriously. One minute, just one second, late and our company would lose its opportunity to make its case for a substantial project. Three million in research down the drain. All my fault.

In those years, the Missile and Space Vehicle Division was located in a former warehouse on Chestnut and 39th Streets, few windows and long rows of pale green partitions. On my first morning, once I'd signed in at Security—some fool in the FBI had given me a Secret clearance—and a couple of engineers shook my hand, they asked me to toss a paperclip over one of the partitions. "What?" I said, looking down at the metal loop in my palm and feeling like an idiot. "Why?"

"Go ahead," they urged in a chorus of whispers. "It's only a paper clip."

So, I tossed and immediately, from behind the partition, there was a great crash and clatter of empty metal containers. The engineers roared. Several more emerged to slap me on the back as they staggered with laughter. I was initiated. This was space-vehicle humor.

The Navy project the proposal would bid on was called Subroc, and it didn't take a rocket scientist to figure out that it had something to do with missiles fired from a submarine. That, however, was the extent of my technical grasp. With no math beyond trigonometry, I found the text impenetrable, all vectors and graphs and formulae with Sigmas and other strange symbols. It was all a magnitude of complexity beyond a ship's turbine. I didn't dare edit a line. I could change a "which" to a "that" and have the whole thing blow up in my face.

My function was coordinating, working up a list of all the material to go into the proposal and finding out which engineer was responsible for it, then compiling the data. That meant begging the man to relinquish his pages despite his professional compulsion to tweak until the last possible moment. These were men in their forties and fifties who had been working days, nights, and weekends for months, strangers to their wives and children, growled at by their dogs when then slipped in from the garage at midnight. One PhD in physics begged me for a few hours extension so that he could attend a Sunday birthday celebration for his mother-in-law: "I haven't had a day off in six months. My wife threatens divorce." I gave in and let him go.

The fact that the proposal was classified *Confidential* complicated my life greatly. It meant that every page had to be logged in, every transfer of paper from one place to another documented, all of it sorted and locked in a secure cabinet each night, then unlocked and re-distributed the next morning. The process took several extra hours each day. I learned that the reason for the classification was a single photo of a jet engine. Several months after we finished and delivered, a picture of the same engine, from another angle, appeared in *Life*. But that one photo, as it were, spread its aura over every other sentence, drawing, or picture in the proposal. It was all Confidential now, and once the military classified, it was impossible to declassify. We were in a Cold War.

About two weeks after I arrived in Philly, Weldon Dick sent two artists from our layout department, Les and Tony, to design the proposal's pages one by one. In those days, artists did rough sketches on tracing paper and then actually cut and pasted typeset prose and graphics on cardboard to be photographed for offset negatives. The several hundred pages of the core proposal would be laid out, printed in two colors, and bound in blue leatherette hard covers. The thousands of technical support pages would be multi-lithed and placed in matching binders. The plan from higher up, we assumed, must have been to awe the Navy's decision makers with a one-two punch of elegant formatting and solid science.

By that point, we were working one-hundred-hour weeks with the deadline looming darker and closer with each second, Les and Tony bugging me for material and me bugging and begging the engineers. It was mothers-in-law and marriages be damned.

Breakfasts and lunches were gulped. Our only break in the day was dinner in a restaurant, an hour or so of calm before returning to our desks and drawing boards. One evening, Les, a frail man with bags under his eyes, left the table for the men's room and didn't return for quite a while. Tony looked at his watch, and I went to look for Les. There he was passed out on the floor tiles. An ambulance came in minutes to rush him to the closest emergency room. Tony and I paced, but the doctors diagnosed only fatigue.

First thing in the morning I called Weldon Dick and reported in a tone meant to shame him, "Les collapsed from exhaustion last night. He was taken to the hospital."

"He hasn't been working that hard," Mr. Dick muttered.

Somehow we finished. Every section wheedled from an engineer, every graphic in hand, every page designed. Too late for an airplane, I was to take the midnight Saturday train from Philadelphia to its last stop in Albany, and then a cab to Schenectady at dawn so that the printing plant could begin its double-time production. I carried all the pages in a large leather artist's portfolio so stuffed it wouldn't zip closed, and Tony ran alongside on the platform as the train pulled out to shove revised layouts at me.

I soon discovered I was on the equivalent of a milk train, this one for Sunday papers, jerking to a stop at every dinky town north of New York City as conductors tossed off bundles of *Timeses, Newses, Mirrors, Tribunes, Journal-Americans*, and other newspapers long forgotten. Those were also the days long before professional basketball players became pampered multimillionaires. In the car with me were the Syracuse Nationals, probably having played the Knicks Saturday and now heading home, very tall and very thin men, all legs and arms, unable to twist into comfort in the—for them—undersized train seats. Their squirming was infectious. My own joints ached as I stared ahead in hollow-eyed sleeplessness.

When I turned in my expense form the next week, Weldon Dick fussed about the cab fare from the Albany rail station even though that train went no farther. "Couldn't your wife have picked you up?" he asked. "It was 5 a.m." I told him. "So?" he said.

The plan had been for me to go home, put all the Confidential pages in the refrigerator in the event that fire consumed my apartment, and then get some sleep after the material was picked up and driven to the printing plant by a co-worker. Everything worked out but the sleep. The phone rang as soon as I hit the pillow. They needed me to explain some things. Another hundred-hour week.

We met the deadline. Hurrah. But no one took time to celebrate. A long shower and it was back to ships' turbines and Mr. Wardlaw. We didn't get the Subroc contract.

But there were other proposals. In the next year, I went back for a month in a Philadelphia hotel and hundred-hour work weeks several times, producing

thousands of pages on potential technologies for sur-
face-to-air missiles, air-to-surface, surface-to-surface.
Ranges, velocities, propulsion, trajectories, effectiveness
probabilities. Only once in all the convoluted prose did
words emerge that gave an indication of what purpose
these devices served. Writing about a weapon called
"Mauler," the engineers estimated "kill power." "Do
you really want to say that?" I asked, assuming a taboo
had been violated. They just shrugged: "Why not?"

Though the cast of characters shifted somewhat
with each project, everyone was looking more haggard.
The offices were as crowded on Saturdays and Sundays
as they were Monday through Friday, the only difference being that the men wore sport shirts instead of
suits and ties. I never asked, and no one mentioned the
status of their marriage. Perhaps they had forgotten all
about their wives and families.

The Mauler proposal ended up twice as big as Subroc, with no time for Les and Tony to dress it up in a
customized layout. Just getting the pages on and off
press took all our energies. What emerged from the
bindery were twenty volumes inserted into a two-foot
wide maroon-colored case, one hundred sets of them.
Seeing them completed, all stacked on the loading
dock of the printing plant, I sighed and wondered if I
would have the energy for a hot shower before sleeping through the next day-and-a-half. But Weldon Dick
stopped me before I got to my car.

"We have a delivery problem," he announced. The

situation was this: It was late Friday afternoon and the proposals had to be at Redstone Arsenal by 3 p.m. Monday. In an era before FedEx, no commercial shipper would guarantee meeting that deadline. But Dick, manager that he was, had a solution: four of us—three others and me—would be plucked from our desks, ordered to drop all other work, and drive them from Schenectady to Huntsville, Alabama.

Donald Nunn and Rick Drummy were given a van from the company motor pool, while Walker Clairmont and I ended up with a wallowing old Chevy station wagon that rattled even when parked. And so, we started off, fifty red leatherette boxes behind us stacked to the roof of the station wagon, another fifty strapped to a skid in the van, each box thick with words, graphs, and formulae. For hours I dozed on and off, opening eyes when my head vibrated against the window and then snoozing again, finally waking up when it was dark and we were somewhere in Maryland. Even though Walker was driving, I was the one to notice the lights flashing in the side mirror. At first, I thought the surges of glare came from high beams pitched up and down by a washboard highway; then I realized the road was smooth blacktop and that our station wagon was wallowing. The car behind was signaling a warning. An elderly man in a tweed cap got out of a grey Lincoln and joined us at the back of the station wagon as we searched for some sign of a problem. "You boys are overloaded." The man put one foot on the bumper.

"Too much weight in the rear. Can't you jettison some of that stuff?"

"Afraid not," I told him. We crept to the next gas station and pumped more air into the tires.

The van was miles ahead, but we had agreed to meet at a hotel in Tennessee, where Donald, a by-the-numbers guy, insisted that we unload both vehicles into our rooms because the proposals were *Secret*. Weary as I was, I didn't sleep all night, shaken by the vibrations of semis roaring past on the two-lane highway. At dawn after a quick cup of coffee, we reloaded and labored up the inclines of the Appalachians, staring at our watches. By noon we were in Alabama, by 2:45 at Redstone Arsenal, and by 3 we had a signed receipt. The Mauler proposal had been delivered on time. We did not get the contract.

By that point in my young life, it was time to do my six-months active duty training for the National Guard, that as an alternative to being drafted for two years. I was about to leave the industrial for the military. Yet there were still six weeks to work on my last proposal, this one for a weapon called "Phaeton," and this time the work was to be done in Schenectady, not Philadelphia. Moved out of my apartment, my wife with her parents in New Jersey, I was sleeping in a room at the YMCA but living at the office, showing up at work by 8 in the morning and going straight through till midnight or 1 or 2 a.m. Then I'd eat a tenderloin at a Toddle House and cross the street to a few fitful hours in my room in the Y. It became a ritual.

Material for this proposal was to arrive from GE facilities in various parts of the country, and I was on my own for all the traffic managing, Weldon Dick gritting teeth on his cigar when I asked for help. "Can't be done. This is a very busy time."

The Secret classification drove me nuts: all that logging in and locking out and locking up at night. It took an hour each night to put the stuff away and another in the morning to arrange it the way I needed just to keep track of what I had. One night, at 2 am, barely able to stand up, I shouted to the empty office, "I can't do this any more!" And so, instead of locking up every page, I tore large sheets from a roll of brown wrapping paper and spread them over the Secret papers laid out on every desk. Then I turned out the lights, locked the door, and trundled off to the Toddle House.

The next morning, I expected to be handcuffed by Security, hauled off to the federal prison where they locked away all the security leaks. But no one seemed to have noticed despite the fact that the night guards probably had never seen desks tented with sheets of brown paper. Perhaps they didn't want to know what they would find if they looked underneath. Perhaps they had orders not to. A deadline is a deadline.

We made it. Somehow we always managed to make the deadline. I had a feeling that maybe this time we would get the contract.

A week before I left for my months in uniform, a

manager in another department, an old GE hand, some-one who once had been as callow as I, sat down at my table in the cafeteria. I asked him about our chances. He shook his head. "Not this one."

"How can you be so sure?"

"Common knowledge. These things are decided in advance. Long before anybody submits a proposal. We never had a chance for Subroc, you know. General Dynamics has an empty plant the Navy paid for. And besides, it was their turn. Raytheon got Mauler. Word is that it's Lockheed for Phaeton."

"Then why did we bother?" I said. "All that money invested, all those people putting in all those hours. Me."

"That's the way things work. We submit proposals so that the military can claim it considered options. Every once in a while, our turn comes up."

Within weeks I was straining at chin-ups, marching through mud, crawling under barbed wire while tracer bullets flared over my head. After finishing my active duty, mired at the lowly rank of Private E2, I didn't go back to GE. The military-industrial complex had to manage without me. Eventually, three decades later, the Berlin Wall was demolished, the Soviet Union collapsed, and our side won the Cold War.

But I had nothing to do with it.

THE WAY THE WORLD WORKS

I HAD TO LIE TO GET into the National Guard. It was either mendacity or being drafted for two years' active duty in the regular army. That was back in the days when military service was inevitable for males who weren't 4F or fathers. I was neither then. It was also a time when a college degree was a rarity. So, at age twenty-two, with the draft board breathing down my neck, I told a National Guard recruiter that I wanted to take advantage of my BA and become an officer. He snapped me up and put me at the top of the list. What I really wanted, of course, was a minimal dislocation to my life—six months' active training and five and a half years of weekly meetings.

I was living in Schenectady when I signed up, working as an advertising and sales promotion trainee for General Electric, coordinating the production of proposals for massive weapons systems. Considering the hundreds of millions a contract would be worth, I had an important function in the corporate world, even a modicum of prestige. Then one day an Army barber buzzed my hair, a sullen supply sergeant tossed a uniform at me, medics pierced both arms with inoculation needles, and taut noncoms in starched fatigues shouted a barrage of commands and curses. Everything was double time, me swept along with a group of dazed neophytes, stumbling across dirt fields, in and out of buildings to accumulate boots, field packs, canteens, tent halves, foot lockers, and M1s.

By the next morning, the chill January days at Fort Dix became packed with push-ups, squat jumps, close order drill, long marches, group chanting, chin-ups, grainy films in steamy rooms, viscid food, infrequent latrine breaks, and hours of polishing boots and buckles and rifle barrels. Every waking hour, noncoms with thick drawls insisted we were human garbage. I hated it. For the first time in my young life, I understood what it meant to lack the luxury of choice. If I so wanted I could have dropped out of school, quit my job, divorced my wife, run away from home. But for six months sadistic strangers would control my every move. How could I endure one hundred eighty days of it?

To make it worse, my training would be for the infantry. As the National Guard recruiter explained, that was prerequisite for becoming an officer. While the others in my platoon would, after basic training, go on to easy days in the signal corps or the cavalry, I faced an additional four months of obstacle course tracer bullets, brambles, mud slime, and freezing nights in a pup tent.

And I was infantry despite my complete lack of qualifications for that calling. Standardized test results verified my unsuitability. Shortly after our arrival at Fort Dix, we were given a battery of aptitude tests at the induction center. I had to answer questions like, would I rather be a machine gunner or librarian. No

contest as far as I was concerned. Results indicate that I
was off the top of the scale for clerical skills and a steep
descent below the bottom for combat adaptability. But
as an officer in the bud, I had a less-than-zero chance
of a changed assigment.

My performance in advanced infantry training left
much to be desired. The day we went to the rifle range
for official M1 rifle qualification, I suffered an allergy
attack, with eyes so watery I could barely see the target.
Pollen was lower on the days I fired the Browning automatic rifle (BAR) and the 30-caliber machine gun. Some
document buried deep in the innards of the Pentagon
must attest to the fact that I am a qualified marksman
for both. For decades, I have been assuring friends that
I will defend them in the event of an enemy attack if
either weapon is within reach.

But otherwise I was a dud. Despite my adequacy in
using the BAR, left-handedness and limited fine motor
control frustrated my ability to disassemble and reas-
semble the weapon That is, I could get it apart. It was
finding the proper place for all those springs and bits
of metal to put it back together that stymied me. I remember one day sitting in a clearing with leftover parts
while a lieutenant standing behind me stage whispered
to sergeant, "And he's a college graduate."

Marching was another challenge, Sgt. Rosa constantly poking at me with a swagger stick and yelling,
"Your other left! An even greater humiliation happened
when the company left me behind the day of the physi-

cal training contest with our archrival, Company D. A flop at push-ups, a dud at squat jumps, I was assigned to guard the barracks.

Clearly, I was a misfit.

But not only did no one in command pull me aside and say something like, "We've come to our senses. You're being transferred to the base library," they looked at me as if I were something nasty stuck to the bottom of a spit-shined boot. And Master Sgt. Dodson, who ran the company office, terrified me—a huge, very black man with massive shoulders and a stalking walk who snarled his words at ninety decibels. One morning, Staff Sgt. Bell ordered me to deliver a report, and I had to tap on Sgt. Dodson's door. "What in the hell do you want, soldier?" Rising from his desk, hulking, lumbering toward me with a sneer, he snatched the sheet of paper from my hand. "Get the hell back to your unit! On the double!" I ran helmet thumping atop my head.

It was no life. Ineptitude, pain, fatigue, fear. I loathed it.

Then one lunch, I happened to sit at the same mess hall table with the company clerk, a short fellow with thick glasses and a soft voice who gave the appearance of being very intelligent despite his baggy fatigues. And he was—a doctoral candidate in math at the University of Chicago. "My time is up next week," he told me, without any indication of pleasure, as if the very notion of time were a problem part of his brain was solving at that moment "So who will be clerk?" I asked him. "Can you type?" he said. And with those words, my military career was transformed. I had blundered into the realm of my aptitude.

To say that I could type was nowhere as big a fabrication as the claim that I wanted to be an officer, but it was a stretch. A high school course left me a rudimentary touch typist, several errors on every line, though not quite as inept as I was a assembling the BAR. To my surprise keyboard skills were as rare in my company as college degrees were in the National Guard. I became Sgt. Dodson's clerk and within days had the veil lifted from the illusion of Army life. I saw how things really worked.

First of all, Sgt. Dodson winked. The second day I was seated behind a manual Underwood while the rest of the company grunted over an obstacle course, another trainee who could have been my doppelgänger— voice cracking, hands quivering knocked on the door to deliver yet one more sheet of paper from Sgt. Bell. Sgt. Dodson roared abuse, made the poor fellow tuck his shirt in, blouse his trousers over his boots, neaten his laces. Then he looked back over his shoulder and gave me a high sign. I gulped and pounded keys. His viciousness was all an act, daylong performance art.

As miserable a typist as I was, he never yelled at me. The morning report, a triplicate form with carbon paper that gave headcount figures in various categories, could contain no more than three corrected typographical errors. Even though I worked as slowly and carefully as I could, I found it difficult to limit myself to three, some days ruining several forms and taking an hour to do a five-minute job until I got it right. All Sgt. Dodson said was, "With the paper you're wasting, the Army could buy another tank."

Sgt. Bell, the *bête noir* of the barracks, for whom no boots were shined enough, no rifle clean enough, no bed tight enough, turned out to be a soft and friendly man who didn't know how to write a check. He approached, almost apologetically, an asked me to fill in the blanks for him to sign, then thanked me as if I had solved the riddle of the sphinx.

Lt. Cole, the company commander, probably forgetting I was in the room, laughing so hard he had to grip a filing cabinet for support, rushed in from one morning formation to tell Sgt. Dodson about Ellis.

"Here is this sad-sack kid," he finally explained when he stopped sputtering, "tripping out of the barracks five minutes after everybody else had assembled with his shirt unbuttoned and his shelter half unrolling from his belt. I began reaming him out, calling him every name in the book, and he just stands there grinning. 'Ellis,' I said. 'I'm insulting you How can you smile?' And you know what he says to me?" Sgt. Dodson shook his head. "He says, 'But I like you, sir.'" With that he began laughing again, Sgt. Dodson with him, the two of them dissolving every time they caught each other's eye.

In less than a week, I found myself growing apart from the rest of the company. Although I still bunked in the same barracks bed and spent the evening hours cleaning boots and rifle, I took no training with them. Their boots were muddy, their rifles stained with use, mine barely used. They began omitting me from their conversations, usually a rehash of the day's struggles in the field and invective about the officers and noncoms. I revealed nothing of what I now knew, telling myself it would be like giving away the end of a mystery. But I admitted, deep down, that I was relishing my secret knowledge.

What finally earned me the others' genuine enmity happened during the weekend bivouac that culminated advanced infantry training. They were to spend three full days in the field crawling through dirt, clambering over obstacles, digging trenches, sleeping in pup tents. To top it off, a hard rain began on Friday morning just as they were about to march out the ten miles to the site. The cadre, of course, would be going with them. Only Sgt. Dodson remained to keep watch over the barracks, with me—his clerk.

We had nothing to do, no morning report, no phones to answer. Sgt. Dodson read the paper and then passed on each section to me. We stood at the window and watched the rain beat against the glass. He drove the Jeep to the PX for coffee and donuts that we shared. He told me how he had met his wife while stationed in Germany. I asked him if he liked the Army. "Sure thing," he told me. "Where else could I get the government to give me housing, medical care, and money every month? In another five years, I'll retire with a pension and I still won't be forty."

"Sounds like a good deal," I said.

"But not for somebody like you. You've got an education. You've got opportunities."

I told him about my time at GE and the weapons systems proposals. He shook his head. "Shit, the infantry never sees anything like that."

After lunch, he carried in the portable phonograph from the day room and put on a stack of Count Basie LPs. All afternoon, we sat listening to music, volume high, the pulse of that tight ensemble resounding through the empty building. He beat time on his desktop, long fingers dancing across the scratched wood. I tapped my feet. Near six, he told me to go home.

"Home, where?"

"Wherever you live. This place doesn't need the two of us all weekend, and I can't leave you in charge."

"You mean it?"

"Get the hell out of here!" He spoke in his growl as he handed me the pass.

When I returned Sunday night in the dress uniform I had worn on the bus, the rest of the company was dragging in from the field, filthy, wet, sodden, mud splattering over the wooden floor. They would have to scrub it clean before being allowed to sleep. No one asked where I had been. No one spoke to me. I was the enemy. And I didn't care. Let them learn how to type.

A few weeks later, my time was up. I finished active duty. Maybe in my six months I didn't learn how to hit a target with an M1 or assemble a BAR, but I had learned how the world works.

The lesson was underlined by a story I heard from a friend from college named Phil whom I ran into during my final days at Fort Dix while gathering the paperwork to muster out. Phil was a Spec 4 in the induction center, stationed there for his two years of service to administer the aptitude tests. He was the one who actually made the training assignments at that base. If I had been a draftee or an enlistee, not pre-assigned by the Guard, I wouldn't have had to spend a day in the infantry.

To exemplify, he told me about Mel, another college friend, who came to Phil in the induction center after being drafted. He asked Phil to find out where he would have basic training. Phil's check of the records showed that Mel was scheduled for Fort Benning in Georgia. But Mel had just begun dating a girl in New York. He pleaded with Phil to get him kept a Fort Dix so that he could see her the weekends he got a pass. Phil asked his sergeant, who shook his head and said he was sorry "These guys," he explained, "are listed in groups of 200. I just can't change things for one of them." But when Phil shrugged and turned away, the sergeant called him back. "Wait a minute. He held up two lists of men. "I can send these 200 guys to Fort Benning and," switching the lists from one hand to the other "keep the group with your friend here."

So, 399 people had their lives manipulated because one had connections. And they never even knew it.

Me, I never did go back to the National Guard unit in Schenectady, and I never rose higher than the rank of private E2. After active duty, I quit GE and got a job in New York. For a year, I had to attend Guard meetings in the New Jersey town where I lived, a tank unit. That's where I gained my MOS—Military Occupational Specialty—as a track vehicle mechanic, although my most intimate contact with a tank was occasionally slapping the metal as I walked past. But that testament to my expertise is probably in the Pentagon too, maybe even in the same cabinet as the evidence of my marksmanship.

I soon moved again and then again, sending in changes of address to the military, the paperwork so far behind that by the time they caught up to assign me to a Guard unit in one place I was somewhere else. Then, after six years, I received an honorable discharge. Actually, being in the Guard wasn't so bad. In fact, it's much like being anywhere. You just have to know the right people.

WHAT WE REALLY DO

AFTER SIX MONTHS OF ARMY BASIC TRAINING, I decided not to go back to being a corporate trainee in the snow belt and took a job as an editor at a small New York technical publication firm I'll call Prestech, Inc. I took it because that was the only offer I had, so desperate I volunteered to cut the requested salary on my resume. In my fantasies, I wanted to write fiction, imagining stories that somehow transcended the inadequacies I turned out on a clipboard in an illegible scrawl. Through sleepless midnights I pondered applying to a grad school that would teach me how to be the real thing. Meanwhile, my fate was work at Prestech.

From a dingy second story loft dwarfed by lower Manhattan skyscrapers, the firm acted as a subcontractor, turning out instruction manuals for large corporate producers of military equipment. In the cluttered, partition-less space, the writers occupied a row of battered wooden desks at the head of the room, the production people sat at workstations in the center, and the draftsmen perched on stools in the rear. The floor was a sea of drab gray tiles, the walls two-toned green, dark enameled on the bottom, pale flat above a middle stripe. Thick pillars propped up the ceiling. People used them for taping up wiring diagrams and calendars and signs like "Thimk" and "You want it when?" Dim light filtered in from the industrial windows on one side of the building, and the powdery odor of blueprints hung in the air. No one, I thought, could feel good about working there.

But I soon learned that didn't matter. Everybody was somebody else, what they did all day for Prestech a triviality detached from their authentic selves, their occupation just filling time till they emerged glorious in their true identity.

Floyd, the squat, toupéed production manager, wrote jacket liners for obscure jazz labels. On weekends, Franklin, his frenetic gofer, donned tweeds and ascot to appraise estates. Jeff, a technical writer with an electrical engineering degree, sought a PhD in clinical psychology, a multi-year project at one course a semester. He was a curly-haired young man, always energized, coaxing the others to reveal their dreams so that he could provide instant analysis. George, also a tech writer, a rangy man with a brittle voice and joints like hinges, invented things, constantly filling out patent applications during the coffee breaks. Leon, the pudgy parts cataloguer, entered expert class bridge tournaments. Natalka, the Ukrainian-born word processor whose blonde ponytail bobbed all day over a Selectric keyboard, took long lunch hours for Broadway auditions. Mac, a grizzled draftsman who looked as if he slept in a cardboard box, wrote torrid adventures for pulp magazines and saved every penny so that he could quit and write a book about the discovery of quinine.

When they asked me what I really did, I—terrified of admitting to my fictions and fearing rejection of the grad school applications I hadn't even mailed—said, "This." Jeff would shake his head in disbelief. "I'm different," I insisted.

Charlie Elman, our supervisor, was a small, round man, bald, with a putty face and a rolling walk, as if the soles of his feet were convex. He sat at a gouged wooden table surrounded by banks of brown file cabinets. Whenever he slid his chair back, he clanked metal. It was Charlie's idea to hire an editor to do all the low-level nitpicking while the writers churned out technical prose. My job was assuring that every section number, heading font, and figure reference conformed to specs.

Most of Prestech's work came through subcontracts from General Electric, mainly manuals for jet engines and defense paraphernalia. Jeff wrote the theory sections, George the operating procedures, and Leon the parts listings. By far, the biggest of Prestech's GE contracts involved a series of manuals for a radar installation with a deadline so distant and a budget so fat that everyone charged time to it but did no work, not with all the other projects stamped RUSH or URGENT. Jeff called it the golden goose, and Charlie fretted for a half hour every month when he saw the billing report, then refocused on the crisis of the moment.

When Charlie Elman—burnt out from deadlines—retired, his forty-year career celebrated with a luncheon tray of pastrami sandwiches, everyone kept saying that he was the best in the business through they had always groused at his commitment to flawless work.

Teddy Madden replaced him, grinning widely as he met the group. A scented man with pink jowls, Teddy dressed elegantly in double-breasted suits buttoned over his expansive middle. He moved through the room pumping hands, slapping backs, laughing heartily, and saying what good things he'd heard about us all. The first thing he did was have everyone pitch in to rearrange Charlie's nest of filing cabinets, giving directions to drag them over against one wall and open up a wide space for himself, a vantage point that let him look out over the whole room. Then, in the afternoon, he interviewed the group one by one, rolling his chair from behind Charlie's table to sit close and overwhelm with aftershave.

When it was my turn, I explained that every day Charlie reviewed the status of my current assignments and checked off a priority list of new ones to come. "He acted as a traffic manager," I said, "and always knew where everyone stood on a project."

Teddy beamed at me. "Well, that's not my style. I like my people to be self-starters."

So now I had to dig up my work, meeting with the writers to find out what needed to be done. My requests confused them, even Jeff. Charlie had always done the planning. They weren't really sure of my function. I ended up collecting their pages and trying to figure out the next step. While my desk overflowed with paper, I spent my time contriving a system but accomplishing little. As time passed, I found less and less to do even though the writers appeared busier than ever. I took hours to sharpen my pencils and neaten my desk drawers. Teddy Madden walked among us several times a day with a radiant smile. When I stopped to beg him for an assignment, Teddy would wrap an arm around me and say, "The world's full of opportunities." So, I took to cleaning out filing cabinets, bundling blueprints and rough drafts for projects that had been completed months ago, dreading the day ahead each time the alarm jolted me awake.

Then, in one of the cabinets Charlie had left behind, I ran across a great stack of material for the General Electric radar project, a timeline stapled to the top folder. Though the contract had started out with a full year for completion, drafts of all five volumes were due in six weeks. Not one had been started.

When I brought the folder to Teddy, I expected his grin to vanish in a panicked grimace. But Teddy just thanked me for calling his attention to the matter and told me to hold onto the folder "for future reference."

A few days later Teddy gathered us all to announce that over the weekend the firm was moving from the old loft to a twelfth-floor suite on Beaver Street, one block from Wall. I showed up there Monday morning and felt that I had entered a movie set. The elevator opened directly into the lobby, where Milly Wolfhurst, the newly hired secretary-receptionist, her aquiline face rich with

makeup, her thin legs arced in spike heels, sat at a kid-
ney-shaped desk in the lobby balancing a white phone in
scarlet fingernails. Each of the three paneled front offices
was furnished with a teak credenza, the largest belonging
to Sidney Preston, Prestech's founder and owner, the one
beside it to his son Calvin, a lean MBA whose major, we
speculated, must have been charm. Because he spent all
of his time on the road polishing clients, it was rarely
used. The third office was Teddy's. Now we had to make
an appointment with Milly to see him.

By this time the radar deadline was only five weeks
away and Teddy was too busy to talk to me. At lunch, I
appealed to George and Jeff and Leon for help in making
him aware.

"Teddy?" Jeff laughed. "Teddy couldn't tell a radar
antenna from an umbrella."

"How do you mean?"

"Teddy hasn't got a clue about technical writing,"
George explained. "He holds schematic drawings up-
side down and makes clucking sounds."

"Then why was he hired?"

"Probably because he smells like Sidney and Calvin," Leon said.

"But who's going to turn out drafts of five manuals
in three weeks?"

All three shrugged. "Don't look at us. We're crazy
with other deadlines. Ask Teddy. That's what he's paid
to figure out."

"Can he?"

Jeff laughed. "Teddy needs directions to order lunch. He's a textbook case."

"Of what?" I asked, but Jeff just winked.

With nothing else to do and a knot in my stomach every time I looked at the radar files, I tried to make sense of the material. Of course, the effort was foolish. Barely able to divide fractions, I'd never even seen half the symbols in the equations, and the technical terms might have been the Rosetta Stone for all the sense they made to me. Still I stared at the papers for hours.

In the midst of my fretting, I noticed one day that Natalka's chair sat empty, her typewriter silent all day, her work undone, Floyd pacing around furiously, dialing the phone, then scurrying to the window to stare out over the street. Past three, she threw open the door and entered, golden hair loose, cheekbones aglow, heels clipping across the floor tiles as she hurried straight to Floyd's desk, leaning forward with an urgent look. He nodded gravely at each sentence. Then she pirouetted with a swirling skirt and rushed back to the entrance. As she opened the door, she turned, threw open her arms, and disappeared.

Jeff told us the news. Natalka had gotten a part, not just any part, but a part in a Broadway play. I expected an enthusiastic outburst, her success verifying their aspirations, an omen of eventual fulfillment for all. But they only muttered, "That's nice" or "Good for her."

"Shouldn't we buy her flowers or something?" I said. "Why not all get tickets for opening night?"

"I've got a big test coming up," Jeff said. "A major tournament," Leon added. "I'm on the verge of a breakthrough and need every spare minute," George announced.

They went back to their desks and never mentioned her part again. But in the days that followed, I felt odd hearing someone speak her name, as if she had become the kind of person you read about in newspapers, not someone you work with.

Two weeks before the radar manual drafts were due, Teddy Madden slid a chair from across the room and straddled it backwards at my desk, his smile broader than ever. "Pack your bags. You've going to Syracuse."

"What?" If he'd said Ulan Bator, I couldn't have been more startled. "Why? What for?"

"That's where General Electric manufactures its radar systems. You're going as Prestech's representative."

"To do what?"

"Their engineers want to update us on some last minute details."

"I don't know anything about radar. I'm only an editor. An English major." I clamped hands onto the arms of my chair.

"You're the one with all the files on this project. I'd say you're the closest thing to a radar expert we got."

Then he was gone and I ran to the men's room, expecting to throw up, but just knelt over the toilet, clammy with sweat. When I stood at the sink, splashing my face, Jeff came in and shook my hand. "Congratulations."

"For what?"

"For discovering your true calling."

"Help me," I pleaded.

He shrugged. "You know as much about radar as I do."

As much as I kept telling myself, *don't go*, I didn't type out the letter of resignation I revised over and over in my head. How would I pay the rent? I showed up in the office the next morning for one more hopeless sort through the project files. That afternoon Milly stepped off her carpet to hand me my plane ticket as if delivering the Hope diamond. "You'll have to get to LaGuardia by bus," she said, the words squeaking through her sinuses. It was to be a one-day trip, out at 6 a.m., back by 8 p.m.

The propeller whine jarred my teeth as the plane lurched through air pockets for the whole flight to Syracuse. I half wished for a crash, a gentle one, where the plane would glide onto the white snow cover that filled the miles below my window. I'd lie warm in a life preserver until the rescuers came and carried me home. I'd never see the General Electric plant; I'd live the rest of my life on the insurance payment and never have to go back to Prestech. But the plane landed right on schedule, and I stepped out into a fierce blast of icy flakes.

A cab took me directly to the guard house at the General Electric gate, where I sat rubbing my ears with my gloves until an engineer named Russ Wenerd met me in a company car for a drive deep into the innards of the works, winding among huge metal sheds and plastic domes.

Russ Wenerd was a man in his forties, a calm pipe smoker, slide rule sticking out from his jacket pocket. When I asked if they always had so much snow, he launched into a recitation of inches and feet and records and degrees, half boast, half lament. It struck me that if I could keep the man talking about the weather, he might forget to ask about the radar manuals. But as soon as we parked outside one of the domes, Russ dropped the subject in midsentence and said, "I'll show you how the prototype's coming along."

"Great." I swallowed. "I'm eager to see the real thing after reading about it for so long."

Russ swung open a steel door and pointed to a metal stairway. We climbed to a ramp halfway up the dome and I saw the shaft of a huge scooped dish poking through a slit in the roof. The shaft looked dark with grease as it slowly rotated with a muffled rumble of gears. From the ramp I looked down at a platform on ground level where three men sat at a bank of green screens surrounded by racks of electronic equipment. Russ waved to them and they waved back. I waved too.

I listened to Russ's praise of the radar's precise sensitivity, its ability to register the subtlest behavior of moving objects. My eyes followed Russ' hand as it pointed out details above and below, comprehending nothing and feeling like an idiot for being so silent, afraid the simplest question would expose my fraud. So, I just nodded and jotted down the few words I understood.

In his office after the tour, Russ lifted a stack of papers from a plastic chair and motioned me to sit for a cup of coffee. "The operation looks pretty impressive," I said, surprised at the words coming from my mouth. "Prestech is happy to be playing a part in this project."

Russ sucked on a pipe that had gone out, a frown crossing his face. Here it comes, I thought.

"I know we haven't been in touch with you people for months," he said. "How many has it been?"

"Five." I made up a number.

"It must drive you crazy to have to work with customers like us. The truth is, we got so hung up with tinkering that we forgot all about the manuals."

So did we, I almost blurted, but instead thought to say, "It's us. We should have contacted you sooner."

"No. It was our responsibility. I feel awful about all the hours you people have spent on the submission using those original documents when we've been redesigning everything the whole time. Look at this." Russ pulled what must have been a thousand-page loose-leaf from a drawer and flipped the sheets. "All engineering changes. You should have had this data months ago. But we kept fiddling, dragging out feet, unwilling to let go."

At first I blinked confusion. Then what Russ was telling me finally sank in. My heart pounded. "You mean we've had the wrong information? That any manuals we delivered in two weeks would be obsolete?"

Russ banged his pipe on his heel, ashes fluttering

to the floor. "That's about the size of it. Our fault, our fault entirely. What do you think?"

"About what?"

"How we can get around this mess."

"We'll need more time." I almost shouted the words, clinging to the seat of the chair, afraid I might leap up and hug the man.

"No question about that. And money too. What do you say to six more months and another hundred thousand?"

"Sounds fair to me, Russ?" I bit my cheeks.

"That's terrific. Thanks, thanks a million." Russ pumped my hand. "To tell you the truth, I've been dreading this meeting. I expected you to be ranting, to throw something at me. I know how I feel when months of work goes down the tube."

"In our business, Russ," I told him, "we get used to the unexpected."

The next morning, on the subway to the office, I had a fantasy of everyone gathered about Teddy's desk cheering my name, Sidney popping a magnum of champagne, Calvin pouring, while Milly Wolfhurst giggled as the bubbles pinged her nose.

But Teddy and both Preston father and son were out for the day. I told Milly what had happened in Syracuse. "That's nice," she said and extended her long fingers to pick up the phone.

In our office, no one was working, George filling out a patent form, Jeff reading a textbook, Leon shuffling cards, Floyd humming and tapping out rhythm with a pencil, Franklin leafing through an antiques catalogue. "They believed me," I announced. "They actually thought I knew something about radar. GE's extended the deadline and they're giving up more money?

The others barely looked up. "Things always work out," George said. Jeff shook his head. "Somebody's still got to write those manuals. It's not going to be me."

A few days later, Teddy did stop by to say, "Good work." He took the files from me and stuffed them back in a drawer. Once again people began charging their time to that budget line.

Not long after, to my amazement, one of the grad school applications I had submitted was accepted. I said nothing for several weeks, until I made plans for a move to the Midwest. Then I gave notice. They organized a farewell, sending out for Reuben sandwiches and cream soda. People shook my hand. Teddy couldn't make it that day. Milly gave me my last check and made me sign some forms. Standing close to her, I realized that she was actually a homely woman.

During the third week of classes, studying day and night from fear of failure, I received a letter from Jeff. Prestech was out of business. I was lucky to have been paid. The next week all the checks bounced. Beaver Street had been a terrible mistake, an overextension into the high rent district. Everyone blamed Teddy. They were all desperate for new jobs. He didn't mention what had happened to the radar manuals.

And Natalka. She appeared in a Hirschfield drawing on the front page of the *Times* entertainment section, between two well-known performers, inked lines accentuating the curves of her nose, her cheekbones, her calves, a Nina at her hairline. Her play opened on a Wednesday, closed on a Thursday. The review was devastating — the script, the direction, the lighting, the acting of the two principles. Natalka wasn't mentioned beyond a sentence that the maid had no speaking lines, just on and off stage with the demitasse.

Late in the spring semester, on a break from grinding in the library, I flipped through the *Village Voice* and found a note about Floyd. He had invented a no-tip coin, roughly the size of a quarter, stamped with "The Service Was Lousy."

That was the last I ever heard of my Prestech co-workers. But then, I'm not up on the latest in restaurant gratuities, clinical psychology, championship bridge, patents, antiques, quinine, or even the Broadway theater. Who knows? In some realm they all may be famous. I wonder if anyone anywhere ever wrote those radar manuals. It certainly wasn't my calling.

HOW I BECAME A COLLEGE PROFESSOR

I BECAME A COLLEGE PROFESSOR because I didn't want to be a corporate executive.

Today, in the second decade of the 21st century, that must sound like arrogance or delusion, what with so many college graduates working as baristas or retail clerks under a lifelong burden of student debt, what with so many PhDs adjuncting at poverty wages and surviving on food stamps. But it wasn't like that in the mid 20th century, when a man with a BA was assured a future of professional success and creature comforts. In those days a man really had to make an effort to be a failure.

I am convinced we were the luckiest male generation America, perhaps the world, has ever seen, too young for the Korean War, too old for Vietnam, spilling out of classrooms into a booming post-World War II economy hungry for managerial functionaries. Corporations grabbed us as fast as they could.

Woody Allen once said that ninety percent of success is showing up; but he left out the most important criterion—showing up at the right time. Ultimately, the life we fall into is all a matter of luck and timing. Don't believe those who claim full credit for their social and economic status, those who argue they deserve all they've got and resent having to part with any of it, as if tax cuts are their right.

When I did my six months of National Guard training, the first week at Fort Dix I underwent a battery of aptitude tests that proved me unfit for combat. Of course, I was assigned to an infantry unit, until—as luck and timeing would have it—I ended up at a mess table for lunch with the company clerk, a studious-looking young man about to muster out and return to graduate studies in math at the University of Chicago. I asked who was going to replace him in the office, and he asked if I could type. Poorly, I told him, but that was good enough. I spent the rest of my active duty behind a desk pecking away at a manual keyboard.

If I had been born, say, a dozen years earlier, I have no doubt I would never have escaped the infantry, clerical aptitude or not. Given my documented combat incompetence, when even the best-trained soldiers were slaughtered on D-Day, I envision myself as one of those khaki-clad bodies bobbing in the currents on a Normandy beach. Instead, my active duty career ended up listening to Count Basie records with Sgt. Dodson while the rest of the unit was out bivouacking on chill, muddy weekends. Timing and luck.

::

In my final college semester, I had to think about

what I would do next, uprooted from the contentment at living in a fraternity house, reading books, writing papers, and hanging out with friends. Besides, I was engaged, about to be married. Soon I'd have a (first) wife to support. Fortunately, recruiters came to campus, and I ended up one of several classmates hired by General Electric, in my case as an advertising and sales promotion trainee. Being hired by GE was a plum job, paying more than most other starting positions and assuring a future of advancement and affluence. Classmates congratulated me, perhaps envious.

When I was considering what kind of job to look for, I had assumed my roles on the college paper and the college humor magazine would translate to a career in advertising, where I would be paid to be clever. So, I envisioned myself a Mad Man, long before that TV series existed as a cautionary tale. Instead, I went to a corporation in Schenectady rather than a street in Manhattan. Graduate school didn't even make the bottom of my list of possibilities. If my thoughts about careers had been graphed, grad school would have come out even lower than combat adaptability.

But what did I know about work? Many of today's college students have opportunities for internships in professional surroundings. My undergraduate-year jobs had been bussing tables at summer resorts and sitting behind a cash register at a co-op bookstore. In adolescence, at fourteen, I did have a one-day career as a busboy but spilled water into the lap of a woman at the first table I served. Next day they put me in the kitchen to clean shrimp; but I was too fastidious about removing every speck of the dark innards running along the creatures' backs and was fired for slowness. I did make money as a pin boy in a bowling alley during a time before machines automated that career out of existence. Every cent I earned I spent on bowling myself. To be honest, I wasn't a very good pin boy, lacking the stamina to jump back and forth between two alleys like most of my coworkers. The summer after high school and before college, I had a job in the warehouse of a local tile factory, where I threw my back out with lifelong after-effects. The short of it is that if I lived like men throughout most of human history when survival depended on manual labor and wartime skills, my fate would have been a life much nastier, more brutish, and shorter than most.

::

One morning in June 1957, I showed up at Building 23 of the General Electric complex in Schenectady at 8 a.m., twenty-one-years old, never having worked a full day in my life, with no idea of what it meant to sit behind a desk for eight hours in a suit and tie. My bussing experience was just breakfast and dinner, midday free to sit on the beach and flirt. My cashiering was only a few hours an afternoon. My daydreams about an actual job involved income, fringe benefits, and lifestyle, with little thought about the actual work.

That work turned out to be tedious. For our advertising and sales training the plan was to have us shift from one function to another and physically relocate to a different GE city every six months. But my hiring year came during an economic downturn in the country, a fact that had escaped me in my collegiate detachment from the news. Instead of the usual fifty annual trainee hires, I was only one of a dozen. My assignment in technical publications ended up lasting much longer than six months. That turned out to be another piece of good luck.

Four of us sat at desks in a cubicle proofreading operating manuals for ship turbines, assuring that all references adhered to specs, and marking up sheets from IBM Executive typewriters that allowed counting of spaces in each line, with wider letters like "m" taking up more than a narrow letter like "l." The goal was full justification, with the typists who retyped every page inserting fractional blank spaces to achieve a flush-right margin. Because the retyped page was new, we had to proof all over again. Those were the primitive pre-computer days.

My cubicle mates and I engaged in frequent small talk as a diversion from the tedium. At the time I estimated we were actually working about four hours of every eight-hour day, and I worried someone with authority would catch on. We'd all be in big trouble. Instead, it turned out, we were breaking productivity records. Our predecessors in that cubicle must have been even more creative at wasting time.

As much as I disliked the actual work assigned me, what I found even more troubling were the duties of those who became managers after the training period, the future that awaited me. Their primary function seemed to be tracking expenditures to assure adherence to budgets. Salaries rose, homes and cars grew larger, wardrobes expanded, but those men—only men in those days—with advancing careers did little but shuffle paper. I realized I wanted hands-on, actually doing, no matter what that doing would involve. Within weeks as an advertising and sales trainee I came to dread the years ahead.

An aside: the chance that put me in technical publications yielded rewards. After my army half-year, knowing I wouldn't return to GE, I was able to get a technical editing job in Manhattan. That experience, when I went to the University of Iowa, led to teaching tech writing in the college of engineering, first as a graduate assistant and later as an instructor, along with teaching core literature. Unlike my literary peers, I knew how engineers were supposed to write.

Beyond the job functions at GE, the corporate lifestyle disturbed me, basically the strategies devised to control the lives of white-collar employees. It was the time when William H. Whyte's *The Organization Man* became a bestseller. Reading it, I recognized the basis of every ploy used to subject us. To develop our social and sporting lives, we were offered minimal-cost memberships at the Edison Club for golf, tennis, meals, and the nineteenth-hole bar. I went once with borrowed golf clubs and demonstrated my inept coordination. It was my first and last golf experience, little white balls sliced at weird angles. We were supposed to volunteer to write publicity for a local charity and religious group. Hesitant about revealing my lack of spirituality, I did escape by helping a community organization once or twice. Essentially, with activities to occupy our non-working hours and frequent transfers to other locations, the company would become the most stable force in our lives, our fundamental bond. For a steady job and a decent salary, GE would own us.

One afternoon in one of our non-proofing lulls, my cubicle group began discussing the Whyte book, three of us agreeing that he'd gotten the details of how we were being manipulated. The fourth member, Dick, a tall young man with a mat of blond hair, was up from his chair and pacing while the rest of us endorsed Whyte's insights. Finally, he spoke with a look of distress: "Why did he have to write that book? I was happy."

Dick and his wife had decided it made more financial sense to purchase a home than rent, accumulating equity. When they did, he was called aside by a manager a few steps beyond trainee status. "Dick," the man warned him, "I didn't buy a house until I was in my thirties." Cars too had a hierarchy of appropriateness, what models to drive and at what stage in one's career.

By that time, I knew I'd be out of there and could safely regard the system with bemused detachment. Not long ago, a friend from college found a letter I had written him at the time, actually had overwritten, announcing that to his certain surprise I had made a decision to go to graduate school. Of course, I had no idea which university, if any, would take me. But I was still not yet twenty-two and, despite having an even younger wife, was willing to risk my chances in the unknown.

My undergraduate record wasn't distinguished, though I graduated in the upper quarter of my class, which seemed to mean something back then. I'd been reading since early teens and even trying to write fiction. Evenings while my wife socialized with garden apartment neighbors—all GE employees—over barbecues in our common yard, I sat inside with a clipboard concocting strange stories with a pen on sheets of paper. I'm sure the neighbors thought I was as strange as those inept stories, and no doubt they were right. I didn't belong in their world.

If I had sucked it up and stayed, I'm sure my off-the-charts clerical ability would have led to an executive position at GE or some other company. Big office, big house, big car, big salary. Another college friend who did become a senior vice president at several pharmaceutical firms once told me he thought I was too cynical to survive in the corporate world. I would have used the word skeptical. But, if life hadn't offered an alternative, I believe I could have kept my opinions to myself and played the game if that's what it took to put boutique bread on the table and a Beamer or two in a three-car garage.

While I came to GE innocent of what the managerial life involved, I did learn a bit about the hardships of
college teaching from colleagues in the technical publications department, actually about the financial depri-
vations of university life. Several of them had abandoned academia because, when the children came, they
couldn't afford to work for professorial wages.

I didn't know these men well enough to ask about
the psychic cost of what I considered selling out. They
still were academics at heart. One who taught the
post-working hours writing course mandatory for trainees gave much attention to the style of Henry James. It's
hard to imagine a business report with all of those "to
put a fine point on it" qualifications. Another who spe-
cialized in semantics liked to ask questions like, "What
would you rather have—a rare slice of filet mignon or
a nearly raw piece of dead cow?" Yet another enjoyed
telling how he and a fellow graduate student at the University of Indiana were in a competition for who could
enroll in the most obscure foreign language. I recall
High Church Hungarian being one. Is there such a language? Was he having me on?

Despite their example of seeking a refuge from mea-
ger wages, my young mind kept thinking, anyplace but
here.

::

Still, I couldn't apply to grad schools for a while.
There was army training to get out of the way and time

for my wife to finish her degree. After Fort Dix, I got the technical editing job in Manhattan despite letters from GE wondering why I wasn't coming back. In leaving the company, though, I wasn't unusual. In fact, most of my fellow trainees were gone in a few years, usually for other firms or companies, one to return to Georgia Tech to get a master's in engineering. Could William H. Whyte be blamed for writing that book, or would we all have figured it out anyway?

::

During the year of editing I had time to consider where to apply, to take a German reading course at NYU, and to enroll in a non-credit story writing course at the New School. I still didn't know which, if any, grad school would have me, though my GRE scores were decent despite my unfocused undergraduate years.

Most of my applications were to American Studies programs because I liked the cross-disciplinary approach, had even written an editorial in the college paper arguing for what I called horizontal education. My real hope was to be accepted by a creative writing program, of which only a handful existed at the time, unlike today where you can find one on just about every block.

Here again, my life was rewarded by an accident of being at the right place at the right time. My New School fiction instructor was R.V. (Verlin) Cassill, then living in New York and supporting himself by turning out paperback potboilers at the same time he was writing literary fiction. Verlin, the first night of the class of twenty or so, warned people that in his experience a majority would drop out and that they could get a full refund if they did right then. Everyone stayed seated, but at the end of the term, only five of us were left. Most evenings after the once-a-week meeting, Verlin and I would go out for a burger and beer. He lamented the good fiction ideas wasted in the potboilers, and he told me he was unable to give me real advice about the semi-fantasy stories I was writing then, in what he called the E.M. Forster vein. He had no affinity for the approach. But Verlin was going back to teach in the Iowa Workshop that fall and encouraged me to apply. My assumption is that he pulled strings and that I wouldn't have made it on my own.

::

Our plan for supporting my Iowa education was for my wife to get a public school teaching position, a very uninformed and naïve assumption. Everyone's wife had a teaching degree and supply overwhelmed demand. I hadn't even thought of applying for a graduate assistantship before we arrived, or for that matter hadn't really considered if I'd teach after getting a degree, but my technical editing experience put me near the head of the line with a freshman comp section for first semester until one opened up in tech writing the next.

Necessity forced me to overcome trepidation. I was more than reticent in college courses and generally shy in life. For my very first freshman comp class I prepared for several hours and ran out of material after thirty of the fifty minutes, with no idea how I was going to fill a semester's worth of time. My hands were sweating, my voice breaking.

But some weeks later the students had a stereotype assignment, in the first part telling how they thought someone filled an assumed expectation but in the second part revealing how that person was really not like that at all. One of my students chose me as his subject—how my voice boomed that very first class and how I terrorized him, but then I turned out not to be such a bad guy. That convinced me I could fool enough people enough of the time to survive in a college classroom.

::

My year of completing the PhD turned out to be another example of stumbling into ideal timing. My decision to go for the doctorate resulted from not getting an appealing job offer with an MFA, probably because I was blatantly unpublished. Besides, I was content in Iowa City, where life was good. So, I became an instructor at a salary that paid for a two-bedroom apartment, food, diaper rental for two kids, and enough gasoline to get back and forth to campus. In addition to teaching three courses, I took two and sat in on others to fill my yawning gaps in English literature. No GE days of killing time.

A university hiring boom was still going on in 1965, the year I passed all tests, turned in a turgid novel for a dissertation, and received the degree. Schools were actually soliciting me, though none whose letters came were from the East, where I wanted to return. After applying to many universities between Boston and Washington, I ended up with a dozen interviews and three or four job offers, including the one from Fairleigh Dickinson Unversity (FDU), where I ended up for the next half century.

Soon the teaching market snapped shut. If I had been a few years younger or delayed longer in applying to grad school, I would have been one of those wandering in the desert of an academic job drought much like that of today. My own department hired no new faculty members between 1968 and 1986. By 1969, I had tenure. Once again, I blundered into showing up at the right time.

::

For me being a faculty member has had almost nothing in common with working in a major corporation. Although most of my career I put in a seven-day week, much of that time unable to tell whether I was working or enjoying myself. Every book I read, movie I saw, trip I took, piece I wrote fed into course planning or just a comment in class. Living and teaching have been inseparable.

::

Classmates from my then all-male college who did become corporate executives seem happy with the way their lives turned out, too. They certainly made much more money than I did, enough to own at least two homes and retire on a sunny island or a few steps from a golf course. As I said, we were the luckiest generation ever.

Without a doubt many of those slaughtered at Normandy were smarter and more talented and would have made better college professors than I, had they survived to go on to grad school on the GI Bill. And many with recent graduate degrees who find themselves adjuncting for fast-food wages or serving lattes are also more deserving than I. Unfortunately, they are victims of bad timing.

MARKED BY MY STUDENTS

THE YOUNG PEOPLE IN THE FIRST college classes I taught remain the most vivid—still, after all this time. Even if I don't remember a name, I retain a distinct visual image. That may be because I was so young myself, just a few years older than those kids, and with even more to learn than the eighteen-year-olds arrayed in desk chairs before me. Soon, after a few years, my students all became a blur, except for the occasional weird ones. When I cleaned out my office for a post-tenure phase and discovered a bundle of pre-digital grade books from my mid-career, looking down the column of names drew a blank. Not a face, not a recalled moment, nothing. I wonder if any of them remember me beyond a vague shadow of that boring guy who went on and on about Dickens and had no idea they never read past the first chapter. But, of course, I did, I knew.

My initial students were innocent Iowans, most as bewildered by what it meant to be sitting in a college classroom as I was to be in front of one. Then, as I felt more at ease in my role, I confounded them with the in-grained Eastern irony I wasn't even aware of. (A writer friend who grew up not far from the university verifies: "Iowans don't get irony.")

One student did make a lasting mark on me without ever opening her mouth, reforming my attitude and interaction with students for the rest of my career. I have no memory of her name, just Miss Somebody. (In those pre-Ms. days I addressed students as Miss or Mr.) This young woman was slight and homely, shriveled in her chair, eyes locked on the desktop, limbs tight against her as if she were trying to vanish inside herself. Her thick glasses were in a colorless frame, her wispy hair dull and tangled, her expressionless face acned. Nothing about her was appealing, not even an inkling of latent vitality. Just drab.

That was my second year of teaching, she one of twenty or so in a Core Lit course. In those days, because students rarely volunteer to speak in class, I called on them individually by name, as in "Mr. Ecton, what do think John Donne was after when he wrote 'Like gold to aery thinness beat'?" After a gulp, Mr. Ecton would say something like, "Poetry is hard." I'd then follow with, "Let me ask the question this way," and, eventually, as several minutes of rephrasings, if lucky, we'd emerge with a germ of an idea.

My plan was not to let anyone in the group escape my grilling, mainly to fill the fifty minutes and to shame them into reading the assignment. The first few weeks of the term I tried to include Miss Drab, but that only made her stare harder at her desktop and respond with a single abrupt head shake. I should have realized the first time that she was terrified, and my direct questioning was an act of cruelty. Soon I got the message. For the rest of the term I never called on her again, allowing her to take refuge in silence.

But I did think of her often, wondering what it must have been like to be her. I empathized to a degree, having been a shy student throughout public school, too timid to volunteer but, unlike Miss Drab, responding when called on. How did she feel to be in college? Had her parents forced her to apply? Was she equally reticent in the dorm and cafeteria? In class she never interacted with any of the others, never looked up to meet an eye or share a smile. Did she have friends? What did she think about in her loneliness?

For my next teaching decades, Miss Drab became archetypal as a constant reminder to avoid humiliating any student, especially the most vulnerable. Because of her, I understood that my courses—as much as they obsessed my thoughts—were far from the most important activities of my students' lives. For some, it was contest of how much they would get away with. For many, though, the crises of romance, family dysfunction, lack of funds, poor self-image, substance abuse, hated roommates, and life's countless burdens overwhelmed anything I had to teach them, even those who really wanted to learn. I know. As an undergraduate I had been one of them.

By now, Miss Drab would be an old woman. I'd like to believe that she didn't experience a miserable, lonely, and unhappy life, that she had literally unfolded her limbs, cleared her skin, looked out at the world, and brightened her face with frequent moments of happiness. Wouldn't it be pretty to think so?

Beyond having Miss Drab as one of those I confronted four times a week, that particular Core Lit section was one of the low points of my teaching experience. Despite all the chairs being occupied, for me it was like talking into a cave, only the echo of my voice responding. My teaching plan in those days was to come up with a list of discussion questions drawn from the day's reading. With this group I was constantly improvising when the initial question was met with a phalanx of shut mouths, especially when I stopped singling out individuals. "Let's think about it this way," I'd say again and again, the next iteration of my asking no more successful than the one before. It was agony for me and, I suppose, for them. I came to dread walking into that classroom four mornings a week. They certainly weren't deliberately hostile. They were pleasant young men and women doing their limited best, as was I.

One day a friend waiting in the hallway outside the open door for our planned lunch couldn't help but overhear me trying to get the group to comprehend why Pope's "The Rape of the Lock" was funny. "That was the most boring class I've ever heard," my friend told me. It had been for me too.

To my relief I had a different section of the same Core Lit course later in the day in a smaller classroom that exuded vitality. With this group hands shot up left and right, dispatching my question list before half the class time was over. Then we could riff, improvise on the material, allow the discussion to follow its own dynamic. Students were engaged. I was engaged. It was energizing for me and, I suspect, for most of them. In that lively section it's likely Miss Drab would have found easy anonymity in the back row.

One day a delegation of young women from the earlier class—hers—came to my office hours with a lament. "We hear your other section is so good. Why isn't ours?" Their quest was based on the assumption that I had it in my power to make their section better. I didn't have it in me to tell them, "The problem is you. The other class has smarter people."

That would have been cruel. But the contrast of sections taught me several lessons. First, I had no right to blame students for not being smart, at least when it came to the subjects of my courses. Second, the success of a course depended much less on me as instructor than on students enrolled. Even if some of them were bright, what really mattered was the group dynamic, the collective personality of the section. It got so that I could tell on the first day of class how the semester would go. If a couple of energetic catalysts revealed themselves, I knew a happy experience lay ahead. If I encountered a wall of stolid faces, I'd have a struggle to contend with. Of course, over the years there were a few happy surprises in the form of a student who transferred into the section a few days later or others who came intellectually alive. Usually not.

I've had colleagues whose ongoing mantra was a plea to raise admission standards, fantasizing classrooms filled with superior, eager students rapt with attention, eager to offer interpretations and opinions, as dedicated to the material as the instructors themselves. My colleagues craved being in the midst of an intellectual elite, every class they taught as rewarding as a learned conversation with colleagues and peers.

But where's the challenge in that? It's a variation of preaching to the choir. The real world involves the frustrations of trying to reach those in the middle, hoping that you've made a connection, perhaps imparted an insight, even a grasp of aery thinness. A special wonder would have occurred if Miss Drab, for all her rigid silence in the classroom, had been listening carefully, taking in far more than I had realized I had imparted, regaling her grandchildren with tales of her college years, laughing aloud every time she read them "The Rape of the Lock."

BEARDLESS IN MISSISSIPPI

THE SUMMER OF 2014 marked the fiftieth anniversary of Freedom Summer, the media broadcasting many reminders of that heroic time, displaying old footage and photos of brave young people, black and white, who risked—and sometimes lost—lives just for encouraging long disenfranchised people to register as voters. Mississippi was the worst of the South, with its legacy of lynchings, its hulking sheriffs and snarling dogs, its bludgeoned black bodies thrown in ditches. During Freedom Summer I was a graduate student joining protest marches on the campus in Iowa City, far from the nightmare where Schwerner, Chaney, and Goodman were murdered.

Reminders of 1960s Mississippi racism still roil me—documentaries, movies, decades-delayed trials of now decrepit Klan members. Back then, I seethed outrage that such a state could exist in America, that people could be brutalized merely for wanting to cast a ballot or go to school or sit at a lunch counter. Something had to be done. Despite the apprehension, the whiff of danger ahead, I felt compelled to become part of that something. But it wasn't till the next spring, April 1965, that I joined a small group from the university to make a gesture.

The night before we began our drive south to Mississippi I shaved my beard. For days I had been telling myself I wouldn't fear for my Northern liberal look and my Iowa license plates. But, shamefaced, I lathered up and scraped away for what seemed like an hour, the stinging skin beneath my cheekbones several shades paler than the rest of me. When I looked in the mirror, I knew it had been a foolish gesture. The White Citizens' Council would spot me a mile away.

During spring break, a dozen of us—young faculty members and final-stage graduate students like me—had volunteered to help Rust College, an all-black institution in Holly Springs, improve its educational program. How we were going to do that wasn't clear, but we assumed we would come up with ideas once we arrived. When others were putting their lives on the line, the least we could do was help some young people learn. After all, we were teachers.

::

I drove my new shiny red Volkswagen Beetle, squeezing in Karl, another English grad student, and a young assistant professor of higher education named Doug, along with our luggage. VWs in the 60s were not the luxury machines of today. Interior warmth came from a primitive mechanism, devices called heater junction boxes on each side of the car. Metal flaps wired to a knob near the gearshift regulated the flow of hot air emitted from the rear engine. Loosen to open, tighten to close. Except that, even in a car only a few months old, my knob didn't work, wouldn't shut. When we began the trip, I had no grasp of the device's mechanism. The Iowa winters lasted many frigid months, and I never drove distances long enough to build up a substantial amount of engine heat.

But by the time we crossed the Missouri border, the three of us sweltered inside the tiny car—jackets off, shirts unbuttoned, glistening with sweat. And we still had hundreds of miles to go. After hours of polite squirming—having had enough martyrdom for one day—Karl and Doug finally asked if I could do something. I twisted the knob again, ineffectually. So, I pulled over to a gravel shoulder and crawled under the car, with no idea of what I was looking for. Yet I did notice the open flaps over square tubing coming from the back of the vehicle. I thought to push them closed by hand, first on one side of the car, then the other. That did the trick. No more heat. But it did get chilly. Those were the options for all the years I owned that car—all heat or all cold.

::

We stopped for the evening in St. Louis, the city of Karl's undergraduate years, somehow finding our way to old Sportsmans Park for the Cardinals' season opener. Our cheap seats far out in left field, home plate a distant speck, we shivered in jackets much too thin for the frosty night. Even though it was hard to focus on the game and not our toes, we endured the whole nine innings. Perhaps we knew we deserved the distress for our lapse, the distraction of amusement in the midst of a cause. The people who gave us their floor for a few hours sleep thought we were making a heroic journey. How could we admit frivolity? But, by the end of our first day, we had suffered heat, cold, and a restless night on hard wood.

::

Holly Springs lies at the top of Mississippi, not many miles below the Tennessee border. As we drove down Route 78 from Memphis, we felt ourselves in a strange land, great tangles of predatory vines and vegetation on both sides of the road, the landscape scarred by wide, empty flood ditches that would become lethal torrents after a storm. This was not the America we knew, the bizarre topography fitting for the realm we had entered, a land of misrule and violence.

When we arrived at Rust College in the late afternoon to join up with the other Iowa volunteers, several officials welcomed us—administrators, faculty, a few student leaders tapped for the occasion. Formal in their greetings, they were all delighted to see us. The dean, a serious grey-haired woman in a tailored suit, called us all Doctor, even those of us not yet degreed. We could see that they had high hopes for our visit.

The small campus was poor, the budget for maintenance and groundskeeping probably minimal. This was a private college. We wondered how many of the few hundred students could afford to pay tuition, even with scholarships. Where was the money coming from? The place had the look of just scraping by, faculty and staff working for a pittance.

We were fed in the cafeteria, pork and bitter greens, and given beds in the men's dorm, where groups of students slept in large rooms, almost barracks style. Everyone we met was pleasant, as if they had rehearsed, on best behavior for the visiting dignitaries. They kept their voices and their music low, obviously uneasy at our presence. That may have been the reason the college moved us to a nearby motel after two nights. Or the officials may have thought that thin mattresses on metal cots were beneath us. That possibility concerned us. Though thankful for the privacy of a double room, we fretted that the college was wasting funds on our accommodations. We were there to be a help, not a liability.

::

To give that help, we sat in on classes, Karl and I in the literature courses. The Shakespeare class was typical, the instructor devoting the entire fifty minutes to playing scenes from a recording of *Macbeth*, now and then prompting the students to listen carefully to this or that speech. What advice could we offer that nice, earnest man? Give the kids a shot of G. Wilson Knight or J. Dover Wilson? The imagery catalogued by Carolyn Spurgeon?

The minutiae of the variorum edition? This was his way of teaching Shakespeare. Students leaned toward the tiny speaker, ears cocked, desperate to learn.

Those from our group who visited classes in other disciplines had similar reports. They offered minor tidbits of guidance, suggestions to consider this technique for getting students to answer questions or that for preparing quizzes. At the same time, we felt compelled to fulfill the faith placed in us, inspire a transformation, an illumination. But where to begin?

::

Uneasy as I was about venturing outside, I was curious to see more of Mississippi than a college campus. A friend who had grown up in the state told me tales that revised my impressions of William Faulkner. What I had assumed products of a Gothic imagination turned out to be reporting, variations on local actualities—the idiot son brought to town who, when not watched closely, would roll down the car window and clamp a powerful hand onto the wrist of a passerby; the spinster sisters who shared an antebellum mansion and the back seat of a chauffeur-driven Packard but hadn't spoken in decades.

The other Iowans were equally drawn to explore the flat countryside, riding out on the roads that led from Holly Springs into fields and farmland. The Mississippi we encountered fulfilled our expectations of poverty—small paint-bare houses with old wringer washers on sagging stoops, chickens pecking in the scrub grass, tireless cars sunk deep in weeds, scraggly curs snarling fiercely as we drove past, undernourished cattle, acres and acres of open land glutted with thick weeds. We had the sense of driving through a time capsule, back into the days of Reconstruction, only the wrecked machines reminding us of the new century.

Every time a pickup truck closed in behind us on the rutted country roads, we panicked, sure that some deputy sheriff, alerted to our visit, was about to lift a shotgun from its rack and blast away on the excuse of a faulty taillight. But no one bothered us. Perhaps we were small fry, intellectuals too effete and useless to be considered a threat to their way of life.

::

One afternoon, requiring needle and thread to repair a pair of trousers, I made an anxious trip to the town's main street. The woman behind the counter of a dry goods store couldn't have been more friendly and helpful, unblinking at my northern accent. "Yawl come back," she called as I left her shop, the bell over the door tinkling softly when I pulled it open.

::

Another day we were taken to meet an elderly black farmer who had long played an important role in seeking rights for his community. My first reaction was to wonder how he had survived, why the White Citizens Council hadn't dispatched his broken body into a muddy ditch along with so many others.

Rather than that small soft-spoken man, another one struck me as a heroic model, his brother, who strode through the farmyard weeds in high boots, erect, broad-chested, skin glowing like cordovan, casting a fierce eye at us, ignoring our greetings in tight-mouthed silence. I saw pride and arrogance, until someone whispered to me that he was simple-minded.

::

Back in the motel one evening, the Iowa group gathered in one room after dinner, I referred to the back brace I was wearing, a formidable apparatus of leather, laces, and heavy steel rods that held me rigid from my waist to my shoulders. It had been prescribed and constructed at the University's orthopedic clinic when an x-ray revealed that, even though only in my twenties, I was suffering a degenerated disk. To demonstrate the contraption, I rapped knuckles on the metal under my shirt. "Hey," Doug said, "they give me the same thing." He was close to my age, but Allen, a tenured historian a decade older, revealed that he too was wearing the identical brace.

What were the odds that three of a dozen men assembled at random would suffer disks debilitated severely enough to be strapped into the same cumbersome prosthetic? We did discuss probabilities, compared symptoms, but no one said what we were thinking: while our aches received professional concern, supportive devices, the backs of people in Mississippi were still being whipped and beaten and burned.

::

The dean, somehow, found out that several of us had not yet received our doctorates and was clearly offended that we had allowed ourselves to be called "Doctor." We hadn't corrected her when she first used the word, thinking it might embarrass her in front of her faculty and, perhaps, wanting them all to think they were receiving advice from real scholars. Another mistake.

::

Our last night at Rust College, a Saturday, coincided with the formal spring dance, the cafeteria tables removed, the booths pushed back against the walls, white ribbons hung from the ceiling, the bare wooden floor a large dance space. Music came from several speakers wired to a record player. The dean and several faculty members officiated, with the students in formal attire—the men in tuxedos, starched fronts, and black bow ties, the women in pastel gowns. Between dances they sat silently in booths, males and females on opposite sides of the room. When the music started, one tune at a time, the men rose, crossed over and bowed before a woman, who stood and accompanied her partner to the middle of the floor. They danced stiffly, barely touching, and not speaking a word. At the end of the song, the men returned the women to their seats and then retreated to their own booths.

We, the academic authorities, clustered near the door to the kitchen, out of place in sport jackets, gaping at the ritual. Once, in Iowa, I had been invited by several of my students to chaperone their sorority dance at a hotel in Cedar Rapids. Despite white gowns, gloves, and dinner jackets, they spent the evening twisting to amplified rock and roll, the band live, the ballroom raucous. "It seems," Alan, the historian, whispered, "that this is an emulation of a plantation society cotillion."

::

In the morning, dean, faculty, and students lined up to shake our hands and thank us for all our help. But we knew we had been useless in Mississippi. Despite our great desire to do something, we had accomplished nothing. To have done so, we should have known where we were going, what we were doing. Today, African Americans vote in Mississippi. Recently they came out in numbers to block a Tea Party U.S. Senate primary candidate. Many have been elected to local offices. They attend the universities. No thanks to us.

When I got back home, driving straight through, many hours in a cold VW, my year-old daughter screamed at the stranger who picked her up. I tossed the razor, re-growing my beard so that both of us would recognize who I was.

FAIRLEIGH FORTUNATE

IT WAS TIME TO MOVE ON. After five years at the University of Iowa, three as a combination grad student and instructor, I'd completed my PhD and, no matter how much I'd come to like living in Iowa City, couldn't stay because my teaching position was temporary. Yet, the prospect of a position in the nearby Midwest, the notion of a life in the center of the country far from my Atlantic coast roots gave me the agita of isolation, as much as I realized that feeling was an unreasonable prejudice. And I also knew I didn't want to be part of a large English department where I'd be pigeonholed into a career of being, say, the Maria Edgeworth specialist, churning out footnoted articles one after another as if anyone cared. My goal was a college in the east, anywhere between Boston and Washington. Despite a number of alternatives, I ended up in New Jersey, the state of my origins.

When I abandoned the working world for grad school, I hadn't any career plan, focused only on the immediate. The same inability to think beyond the now had prevailed when I moved to Iowa to write, teaching—initially as a graduate assistant—merely a necessity to support myself. It surprised me to realize teaching would be my future and that I had become an academic. But I knew little about the workings of the university world, just as I had been ignorant of what it meant to work for a corporation when I took a job with General Electric after college. Even with five years in the classroom, I had no notion of how a university operated, what it was like to be a real faculty member. At Iowa, I had been assigned to certain sections with the texts and syllabi already chosen, a pawn deployed by an organizational superstructure. The system pointed me in a direction, and I played my role, accepting the assignment as the equivalent of a natural law, a slot in a template emanating from on high.

At age twenty-nine, inured to accepting the authority of successful writers who critiqued my fiction and senior faculty who graded my essays, I still assumed that those with the wisdom of experience led with competence and control. My first inklings of the reality came when I dove into job hunting.

Because I was receiving my doctorate in a bumper year for academic job seekers, the many application letters I typed yielded a dozen interviews, most scheduled into a packed few days of a Modern Language Association conference that took place right after Christmas in a frigid Chicago. Fairleigh Dickinson University (FDU), one of the schools on my list, wasn't sending a representative. After hesitating, I wrote back to arrange an interview during a January break visit to family in New Jersey.

Seeking authoritative advice before Chicago, I met with Iowa's English Department chair, John C. Gerber, an archetypal academic with blue blazer, gleaming teeth, and groomed white hair. He and Mrs. Gerber, also with a white coif, hosted grad student teas at their well-appointed home. She poured, offering a smile and a polite comment with each cup. Dr. Gerber, a model of objectivity, scanned my list of interviewing schools and recited the problems rampant at just about every one, insider gossip. To my surprise, he had no negatives for FDU. Why not? I kept thinking. Why not?

As a New Jerseyian, I well knew FDU's mocking sobriquet, Fairly Ridiculous. Rutgers classmates, needing a core science course and lacking any scientific proficiency, would sign up at FDU summer school and pass with A's. Could it have been that FDU was too insignificant to even register on Gerber's scale of defective universities? I puzzled.

With a train ticket and a hotel reservation in Chicago, I traveled to the convention to appear for two days of interviews in cluttered rooms. In some cases, several were being conducted simultaneously in the same small space, conversations blending. That was the setting for mine with SUNY at Stony Brook. The interviewer, upon learning that Iowa permitted creative work for the PhD dissertation, was stunned. "You didn't write a scholarly thesis," he said. "What could you teach?" I closed the door behind me.

For some forgotten reason, I did schedule an interview not in the east, but with the California university at San Luis Obispo, where there were only two of us in the room, me wanting to be out of there as soon as I entered, knowing I would be wasting both our times.

My interviewer, a pleasant man as far as I could tell, went on and on about nothing but the school's salary scale, how the system of raises and rewards was based on a clear and open formula that left no uncertainties as to where anyone stood. To make my exit, I asked, "Then what would someone like me be making?" "It's hard to say," he told me.

Some of the conversations seemed to go well, though substance blurred. A few schools said they would be in touch. Why not show up for an FDU interview? I would be a short drive from where I was visiting and take only an afternoon.

The first time I passed through the wrought iron gates of the campus, I realized I was not entering a normal university—just from driving up a winding road through a manicured landscape of trees and shrubbery and confronting a large, pillared mansion. It was the grounds of what had been a Gilded Age estate. Then, once inside a marble great hall, I was led into a spacious, wood-paneled office to undergo a job interview with the dean of liberal arts, the campus dean, and the department chair. That interview made the ambiance even odder, the liberal arts dean—an Englishman—mumbled through an incomprehensible British accent. Some tale, I think, about being kidnapped by Indians in Iowa. The campus dean—easier to interpret—went on and on about his vision of college education as if on autopilot. The chair just sat with a benign expression, as if he had come into the middle of a performance oblivious to the plot. At the end, the three shook my hand, and I emerged into the great hall with no idea of what had happened.

The fact that I didn't flee, get in my car and speed out those iron gates without looking back, the fact that they offered me a position, and the fact that I accepted, reveals much. It was a fit for a misfit—FDU and me.

Because my Iowa City apartment lease ran out on May 31, I couldn't stay to walk across the graduation stage to hear my name on June 1. That day I was already in a packed VW Bug with a wife and two toddler daughters, heading east into the unknown of being an assistant professor. Insects splattered the windshield, fogging my view.

A recently unearthed a photograph depicts me in my first years at FDU—dark hair, dark beard, dark-rimmed glasses, button-down shirt, foulard tie, tweed jacket. Very much a cliché academic. When before that photo, in my early twenties, I was cleanshaven, my jaw visible, my glasses still horn-rimmed, some friends—and perhaps enemies—told me I reminded them of Clark Kent with my quiet demeanor. I took that as a testimony of my limitations, not my potential for a caped transformation.

Once my first FDU semester began, I met and liked my colleagues, the whole full-time faculty no larger than a single department at Iowa. Within weeks, I found myself mingling with biologists, chemists, accountants, psychologists, and more. We crowded at lunch tables in the faculty dining room to be entertained by the witty raconteurs. I just listened, nothing clever to offer.

The campus seemed to be run by a small hierarchy

of elders from various disciplines, men—only a handful of women on the faculty—who met at a conference table with the campus dean, Sam Pratt. They made decisions, primarily implementing aspects of Sam's educational vision. For me as a newcomer, they seemed to exude an eminence, at least until I knew better, which didn't take long.

Sam turned out to be a bit of a despot, albeit a gentle one, but so obsessed with his educational vision that it was often difficult to regard him seriously, especially when he let his hair grow long and began wearing plaid trousers in a stab at being trendy. Once he went to a conference and came back with the idea that teaching writing would become obsolete and that students all should be given movie cameras instead. That was decades before smart phones and Instagram. Another of his ideas anticipated students getting library access from their dorm rooms. A visionary so far ahead of his time he just confused the rest of us.

I recall the evening during the first weeks of the school year in which he gathered all the new hires into his office for a heart-to-heart about doing right. One admonition elaborated on the fate of a fired drama instructor a night watchman had caught in flagrante with a student at the back of the theater prop barn. "If the man only had enough sense to spend fifty dollars on a motel room," Sam exclaimed, several times. When the meeting broke up, Alan, a historian, whispered to me, "How does he know it's fifty dollars?" But I couldn't imagine Sam groping a coed.

Just as a few months at General Electric had exposed the flaws of the corporate world—people's tendency to puff up their significance—my first weeks as a faculty member revealed a parallel tendency to self-importance in the higher ups. It was the whiff of authority that led them to accede to self-importance.

Once I was inside the dynamics of the institutional mechanism, it became obvious that those in charge were merely avatars of the Wizard of Oz. I had parted the curtain and witnessed inept hands fumbling at levers. I wasn't in Iowa any more.

Some of the others longer in the academic trenches were aware of this before I caught on. But I was soon in the ranks of the iconoclasts. I found myself more vocal, speaking up at meetings if not the lunch table, conspiring with colleagues to resist the follies of those in charge. Even though untenured, I surprised myself by having no fears of retribution, still living in the now.

At the time, our evening division for part-time students was a separate unit, administered by its own dean, a martinet of a man, given to creating rules and regulations. He even sent out a memo listing the Ten Commandments for Evening Faculty: Don't sit when teaching; don't lean against the desk. And eight more of the same. I couldn't help myself from distributing a version of the 23rd Psalm: "The Evening Dean is my shepherd. I shalt not sit when lecturing. I shalt not incline against the desk. ... Surely, attentive students will follow me all the minutes of the period."

I couldn't help myself, under the influence of my

English department colleagues, a group of cutups—
physically and verbally.

For example, I'd be discussing an essay with a freshman when my colleague Walter Savage would appear
down the hall from his office, stop abruptly in front of
mine, leap to grab the lintel over the open door, draw up
his knees, and slowly swing back and forth. This, a man
in tie, sports jacket, and dress shoes. The freshman would
sit rigid, straining not to look at that dangling man, while
I droned on deadpan, as if nothing unusual were taking
place. Sophomores knew enough to dismiss him with
the wave of a hand. A small sign of academic progress.

Although that Walter (I relegated to be the Other Walter) was clearly the head clown of the English
department, we were all complicit. One year for the
student yearbook faculty photo, we climbed into the
tub in what had been a bathroom, bodies jammed, legs
locked. The students wouldn't print the photograph.
They cropped it, leaving a conglomeration of heads and
faces at odd angles and elevations. That picture cap-
tured the essence, though the tangled tub would have
been more accurate.

We endured through irony, mocking the foolishness
of administrators with parody memos, finding comedy
in student malapropisms ("It's a doggy-dog world,"
"Nietzsche believed the Darwinian theory that man re-
gressed from the apes.") In hopes of revising the turgid,
unsingable alma mater, Bill Zander and I wrote our
own: "Fairly D, O Fairly D; tee hee hee, O Fairly D."
Bill and I and eventually much of the department wrote

chapters of a collective novel called *The Peabodies*, with three siblings based on *The Brothers Karamazov*. I remember Bill's opening line: "'Time to rake the leaves again, gol dang it,' Father Peabody said." We passed sheets of paper to write collective limericks at boring faculty meetings. We formed the Lusitania Film Club to choose the worst possible movies for viewing at Friday night potluck dinners, where we could hoot at the dialogue and groan at the acting.

That's not to say we weren't serious about our teaching responsibilities to students, even those slackers who didn't think they cared and who still ended up learning something. Happily, enough of them did care to make the classrooms tolerable and often rewarding.

Our larks were strategies for coping with irrational administrative demands and decisions, made by people with titles operating by the seats of their pants. After decades in the profession and conversations with faculty at other universities, I discovered our situation wasn't unique. In fact, it's a clone of the blunderings rampant in corporations, governments, and even families. Worse some places, better in others. The flaws manifested when people try to control others and believe their titles actually mean something.

The series of pranks that made up my career at Fairleigh Dickinson did strip away my outer Clark Kent layer to reveal, not a man of steel, not a leaper of tall buildings, just a guy able to plunge into the antic tub. The secret of survival is not to take yourself seriously.

MOoNLIGHTING

FOR DECADE OR SO, although I had a full-time, tenured faculty position, I wasn't scraping by; in fact, found myself digging deeper into a financial pit with each paycheck. To get by, I took on a range of moonlighting gigs I dignified by calling myself a consultant. The tasks involved writing training and procedures manuals and running writing seminars for a variety of industries. I lugged my Lands End canvas case from telecommunications to banking to electronics to supermarkets and even to a conference center. The corporate world operated on a very different pay scale from the academic. Compared with, say, grading a stack of freshman essays, it felt like free money. I wanted to give these short-term employers value for their dollars but had no investment in what they did with my labors. Nothing was at stake.

The Supermarket Industry

Now and again, I exited the Garden State Parkway onto a potholed road that led into a wasteland of warehouses to meet with my contact at the headquarters of a supermarket chain. Karen and I got on well, perhaps because she did her job with a sense of irony, bemused by the irrational decisions of the vice president she reported to and the gamesmanship of her coworkers.

Late one afternoon, she pointed to the row of cars parked outside her office window. "It's like playing chicken," she told me, "to see who will break down and go home first. Who stays the latest wins." I asked her if there was really that much work. "Of course not. People just read the newspaper."

She let me in on the industry's dirty little secrets, like store brands being the same products as the advertised nationals with a different label. She revealed that store managers shrugged when customers complained about finding a caterpillar in a can of corn: if you're going to put billions of niblets in millions of cans, a creature is going to slip in now and then.

I wrote procedures manuals for Karen: how to pack a paper bag most efficiently, heavy objects on the bottom, boxes against the sides; how to create those free-standing product displays that glut the aisles and block carts; how to unload delivery trucks and stack boxes in the stock room. The latter I considered my finest effort, my instructional masterpiece, as it were. The next time I visited Karen for a new assignment, I had to ask how those manuals were doing. There were, she told me, hundreds of copies stacked in a closet. Her vice president hadn't decided when or if to distribute them or perhaps had forgotten they existed. I just cashed the check, long used to writing unread words.

By the way, that supermarket chain is now defunct.

Telecommunications

Like the supermarket company, the one I consulted for in the telecommunications industry no longer exists, both swallowed up by other organizations after making a mess of things. I don't take it personally, blaming the work I did as a cause of the failures. But who knows? It might have been the butterfly effect.

For this company, I both wrote manuals and taught writing seminars. The manuals involved self-instructional training in the workings of a specific industry to prepare members of the sales force to impress the client with how well they understood the way the business functioned and how they just happened to have a multi-million dollar piece of equipment that would increase efficiency, solve problems, and bring about organizational bliss.

For example, on a day I wasn't teaching, I flew out to Cleveland to spend hours with an expert who explained the ins and outs of the tire industry, he talking off the top of his head, me frantically scribbling notes with minimal comprehension. Then I went home and had a few weeks to try to make sense of it all.

I should note that this happened in a time before computers when I was reduced to writing by hand in a scrawl that took special powers to decipher. It was also a time when large organizations owned clunky Wang word processing machines lined in a room with women clicking at keys for endless hours. My handwriting was a cause of despair. The women were pleasant to my face when they asked for a translation of my marks on the page, but they must have cursed me behind my back, haunted by my script on the walls of their nightmares.

Still, they managed to process my words and turn out a manual. The next step was to test it out with representatives of the sales force that would be compelled to use it for their training and, ultimately, their corporate futures. For the tire industry manual, I flew out to Akron, a hub of radial manufacturing. We gathered in a motel meeting room, where things moved along smoothly (I won't say without a bump in the road) until the group got to my stab at demonstrating a formula dictated by the expert in Cleveland. My explanation led to a meaningless calculation. Consternation. I would have to fix it.

My preference would have been to skip dinner and get right to it, but the code of sociability required that the people from the company's Akron office show off their city's nightlife. We were driven to a restaurant and then to a hot spot of that era, a disco. Within, some strange ritual was taking place. Given the overpowering beat vibrating from the loudspeakers, we couldn't hold conversations and just sat at the edge of a large dim room with a large floor space surrounded by little round tables so high that people had to stand with their drinks. When a new record began to throb, men and women paired off in the middle of the floor and gyrated under colored lights flashing across the ceiling. I tried to concentrate on what I had done to screw up that formula; but it wasn't till we got back to the motel and middle of night quiet that I finally figured it out and made the repair.

Most of my manual assignments for that telecommunications company gave me sufficient lead time, though I once got an urgent phone call pleading that I write a case study overnight because someone from a rival department would if the department that called me didn't get to it first. They'd lose power. Why not, I said, and turned the situation into an organizational dilemma that called for telecommunications to the rescue. To dramatize the case, I had to create, such as they were, characters, identifiable people with roles to play in setting up the problem and solution. On a whim, I decided to give them names from George Eliot's Middlemarch: Dorothea Brooke, Bulstrode, Lydgate, Fred Vincy, Mary Garth, Will Ladislaw. But my contact at the company had been an English major and changed them all to equivalents of Dick and Jane.

Writing Seminars

Helping—or trying to—employees improve their writing skills felt much like teaching undergraduates but with very different topics, even duller. My preference was to get advance samples from the people in the group so that I could see what types of writing they were actually doing and diagnose their specific needs – usually "it's" for "its," the point of a memo buried in the fourth or fifth paragraph, and sentences too glutted to parse.

The latter was most true of the examples from a company that manufactured electronics for defense systems, the prose so baroque it seemed to be encrypted. This was the group that asked me to tell them definitively whether there should be a comma before the last "and" in a series. When I told them it depends, I sensed that wasn't the answer they wanted and that they considered my inability to provide an absolute yes or no proof that I had nothing useful to say about the writing process. If one of their weapons had been handy, they probably would have vaporized me on the spot.

The greatest frustration came when I didn't have a client's samples and was reduced to generalizing do's and don't's. One such case which still bothers me involved a bank that still exists, though transformed by a series of mergers. I was to conduct the writing sessions of a week-long international seminar taking place at a country hotel outside Stratford, England, where employees from U.S. and European branches would gather. Even though I visited a lower Manhattan tower to meet with several of the vice presidents—everybody was a vice president—who would be my students and even though they promised, not a sheet of paper ever reached my hands. I had, and still have, no idea for what they did.

Every instinct told me the sessions would be a disaster. They were, my hours standing in front of a hotel

meeting room excruciating, everyone aware I was fak-
ing it. Probably even the desk clerks out in the lobby.
The air suffocated with boredom. Some of the European
managers already were bent out of shape because, to
fill up the complement of students, secretaries had been
invited to come. You could see it in their sneers.

(Pastures surrounded our hotel, once the manor
house of an estate, and the rail thin woman from New
York there to teach speech was terrified of the cows. But
that's another story.)

More regularly, I conducted week-long writing sessions for a branch of the same telecommunications company that asked for the training manuals, this branch
responsible for manufacturing equipment back in the
days when telephones were ungainly black objects,
wired to the wall and built to last 75 years. Over several
years and in several locations around the country, my
students were at first just middle-aged male engineers
and later on women managers and accountants—people who normally spent eight-hour days in cavernous
rooms among rows of brown wooden desks, staring
at blueprints or sheets of numbers, obsessed with their
place in the corporate hierarchy.

The purpose of the week was more effective writing,
almost all of which was internal memos and project
reports, with an occasional letter to the outside world.
Following their examples, I did have them sit for exercises to make them see the importance of a clear and
specific subject line and an opening paragraph that com-

pressed the gist of the message for busy recipients who wouldn't read further. Although I wouldn't think of using the analogy out loud, these openings were much like the beginning of a short story, the one chance to grab the reader.

But enforcing writing exercises on people for four and a half full days would have been a cruel and unusual punishment. (The week ending with a half day on Friday for time to catch planes for home from Manhattan or Hopewell or Lee's Summit or Oak Brook Park or wherever we were, and that half day usually a waste given the woozy aftermath of the Thursday night farewell partying.) So, to break things up, I revised the seminar topic to writing and communication, concocting a list of job-related issues for discussions that would fill the time between writing.

My first-day icebreaker had each person in the group stand in front of the room and explain their job function, a form of introduction. That always ended up as a litany of acronyms: "Our department processes RQTs though the BGOVs to make sure they adhere to GTW standards." Initially, I assumed I, an outsider, was the only one bewildered. But when I asked the rest of the group if they understood, I saw shaking heads. You had to be working at the next desk to get any notion of what the person was talking about. My first lesson in communication.

Another involved cutting a color ad from a magazine and asking people to describe what they saw. Let's say it pictured a bucolic floral field along a sparking river. The engineers would write something like, "In the upper left-hand quadrant there is a thick line of silvery color. The lower right is dominated by various shades of green." Someone else, most likely a person who had majored in the humanities, might say, "Spring! I feel spring! Birds in the air, butterflies, the pristine beauty of a rushing stream." Communication lesson two.

But even writing and communication lessons weren't what my groups really wanted and, I came to realize, what they really needed. They were burning to vent, and most of what they vented about related to the company's hierarchy and their place in it. The layers of management were so rigid and hermetic that employees were forbidden to communicate with someone at a higher level without the intervention of their direct supervisor. The trick they devised was the cc: list for memos. Somehow superiors could be copied but not addressed as the primary recipients. Years later, when the company eventually went down the tubes, its business shrunken, its stock in decline, its name and assets bought out by an upstart, I understood the inevitability, the other shoe dropping.

Beyond hierarchy, there was aimlessness. At one of the venting sessions a young woman in her twenties complained a project she had worked on for a year, her entire time with the company, had suddenly, without warning, been cancelled, the plug pulled. The engineers, men in their late forties and fifties, just laughed. One said, "I've been with the company twenty-five years, and not one project I've been assigned to has ever been finished."

There was a time, right after college, with no better idea of what to make of my life, I accepted a job as a management trainee and, like the majority of my class-mates, might have ended up functioning as an executive in some company. Years later, well into my professing career, I made that speculation to a friend who was a corporate vice president. He shook his head. "You're too cynical." Of course. How could I not be? I'm much better suited to that world in moonlight than in day-light.

WILLIAM ZANDER, 1938-2019

BILL ZANDER HAD BEEN a friend and presence in my life since 1961 when he appeared to take a technical writing instructors' desk in the Engineering Building at the University of Iowa, a tall, very thin young man with a standup crew-cut. That's almost sixty years ago. Since that day our lives intertwined in three states and on one Balearic island.

When Alex, Bill's wife, called the afternoon of April 3, 2019, to tell me that he had died very peacefully, just stopped breathing, I thought I would be relieved. He had been in hospice care for more than a week, agitated initially, then just signaling for water to moisten his mouth and lips, in restless unconsciousness. His wife and sons had taken turns sitting by his bedside, sleeping little, alert for the end. Death would be a release for Bill and for them. I hoped for it. But the fact, the actuality, hit me with a profound and unexpected grief.

Bill was unique, unlike any other friend I ever had, multiply talented, consistently witty, frequently zany, with a distinct way of speaking that matched the meter of his poetry. When our department chair of the time told him his classroom popularity had led to a large following of students, Bill would emulate his vision of that following with a stiff-kneed, arms stretched, zombie lurching down a hallway.

But Bill was also a man of sincere rectitude, a word he liked to use, not for self-congratulation, but because the sound of it pleased him. He had been amused because another chair spared him committee assignments with the belief that Bill was too sensitive a poet to be burdened with the mundane. But when he did find himself on committees, Bill took the responsibility very seriously, just as he did his commitment to students, as much as he clowned in the classroom.

Learning of his death, one wrote me, "Oh no! I loved him!!! I had so much fun in his poetry class. I've often thought of him and his fabulous poetry. One was about getting stoned at a young friend's funeral and another about making a room come to order like Hitler.' Another said, "I was very fond of Bill Zander. He was my mentor at FDU, and my friend of many years. Bill understood the value of exposing students like myself to a wide range of quality writers. He mentored me through my first published chapbook, which he edited, and helped me win thousands of dollars, the ultimate validation at that time for a would-be professional writer."

When asked to teach journalism courses—he had a bachelor's in journalism from Missouri before his master's in English—Bill took a summer job at a local newspaper to learn the then-new digital composition technology to make sure his students would also be up-to-date. But he did disparage his own undergraduate journalism courses, mocking one that did little more than cope with tickertape output.

Bill chose poetry as his artistic outlet, with publications in many literary magazines, two book collections, and one chapbook. But he could have succeeded equally in several creative outlets, and, if not teaching, could have supported himself with a career at Hallmark Cards, his first job after college, where his verbal wit was a perfect match for the company's move to a comic line.

In Iowa City, Bill and his then-wife, Sara Lee, lived in the suburb of Coralville, in the basement flat of a house owned by a medical student with a two-year-old son who constantly played with himself, to his parents' alarm and embarrassment—and to Bill's amusement.

In their Coralville flat, they owned a black and white TV (we had none), where we would, with our then-wives, watch the very limited offerings of 1930's gangster movies that we called "You Sap" movies because of that term's frequent use in dialogue.

They shared that flat with an orange tomcat called Philip (really Philly Joe Jones), who sought out fierce confrontations with rats, returning home with bites and torn ears, and the need for frequent visits to vets. Bill liked to name things. His car at the time was a ponderous, wallowing, pale green DeSoto that he dubbed Henry James. Later, when he taught creative writing, he told his students to call the course Otto, influenced by John Lennon answering "George" when asked what he called his haircut. Bill also was far ahead of other musical critics, publishing an essay on the genius of the Beatles a year ahead of Richard Poirier's much more influential article in *The Partisan Review*.

Beyond writing poetry at Iowa with Don Justice and fiction with Verlin Cassill, Bill played the guitar and wrote songs (my favorite of his lyrics lines comes from "When It's Summertime in Maine": "When the bougainvillea blooms / we will look for furnished rooms"). He also sketched very well and once gave me a book of his drawings that included the elaborate carved-framed Victorian mirror behind the bar at Donnelly's, an occasional alternative to writers' hangout, Kenny's. Bill also possessed an encyclopedic knowledge of jazz. Who else could refer to the obscure clarinetist Alcide "Yellow" Nunez in a work of fiction as if the reader should know who that was?

But beyond writing, Bill's greatest passion then, and throughout his life, was fishing. He introduced me to a fixation on the quest for bites, spending hours on the edge of the Coralville Reservoir or the banks of the Iowa River. We bought lures and bait at Cliff Hoag's tackle shop, where Cliff kept a large spoon-billed paddlefish in a tank. When we bemoaned our lack of catches, Cliff alternated explanations—"The water's too warm" or "The water's too cold," phrases Bill and I used for years to explain what we couldn't understand.

When, after a year and a decision not to pursue a PhD, Bill left Iowa to return to teaching at the University of Missouri, I visited Columbia a few times, and he came back to Iowa City to visit, sampling the home-made saki a number of us were fermenting, and sleeping on the sofa.

When my department at Fairleigh Dickinson had an opening for a poet, I encouraged Bill to apply and accept the offer. Several years later, he house sat and cared for our dog when I spent six months in England during my first sabbatical. The next fall, when he was in Spain on his, I, with family, visited him in Deja, Mallorca, over the Christmas holidays. He introduced me to Robert Graves, drove us around the island in a chartreuse Fiat, helped my young daughters concoct a tree from scraps, and took us to a village restaurant to introduce me to squid, while his dog—Lady Brett Ashley—slept under the table.

Locals couldn't understand why he had brought a mixed-breed hound all the way from the States, often asking him in their puzzlement if she were a valuable animal. But he flew Brett many places over the years, from coast to coast several times. She was a tranquil flyer until some baggage handler misdirected her to Duluth, and she had several days before reuniting with Bill. From then on, she had to be tranquillized.

Brett didn't go to the upstate New York wedding of one of Bill's former students, where Bill was the best man. But I was there too, unaware that among the various introductions of people who hadn't known one another, Bill met Alex, his wife of almost forty years. They hit it off at first sight. When reporting the wedding, the local paper identified the best man as Willard Zarder. Bill loved it, referring to himself by that alter ego again and again.

Bill liked to take long hikes in the woods with Brett and later pet dogs, seeking flights of raptors and spending days on wilderness trails. In his final years, he lived on a lake, splitting logs for a wood stove and taking a boat on the water for fishing. He wrote naturalist articles for magazines in addition to poems, devoting himself to thorough, detailed research, a stickler for the right detail.

He and I often fished together, travelling the state for lakes and streams, he always catching many more than I did, stopping for a beer afterward, where he would invariably do his imitation of a fictional redneck whose yard we had walked through to reach water—"Get offa my property!"

Beyond fishing, we hung out, once to a double feature of Antonioni films—*L'Avventura* and *LaNotte*. We went to jazz clubs that no longer exist, hearing the Dixieland clarinetist Bobby Gordon in Chester and Johnny Hartman in West Paterson. We gave each other gifts of jazz CDs, although Bill was equally expert in country music, Flatt and Scruggs, Ralph Stanley, The Sorry Bottom Boys. (Bill named a group of guitar-playing MFA students The Soggy Liver Boys.)

Just a couple of months before Bill's death, Bill in the audience, his self-defined county punk performing son, Gabriel, sang Bill's song "Does Your Mother Know

You're Sleeping with a Hippy?" to raucous cheers in a local bar, Bill laughing when he told me about it. That was one of our last phone conversations. He always ended a phone call with a bit. Like "May the Good Lord take a liking to you."

Yet for all of his wit and antics and for all of the joy he brought others, Bill was a brooder, confronting shadows that he revealed most openly in his poems, often inseparably from the lightness of their manner. Among the last group he wrote were a number titled with old sayings, like "Leaving Little to Chance" and "What Do You Want for Nothing?" The concept could have been the source of humor, but Bill probed the veiled potential of the clichés, undermined the seeming obviousness of the colloquial. Life, as explored in these poems, yields much more density and uncertainty, the threat of dark loss. That's seen, for example, in the final lines of "Beyond Belief":

> Beyond belief is you, yes, the middle
> Of nowhere, almost at home there, too, as if
> You had built it, though you can't help looking back
> To the place you longed to leave.
> Beyond belief
> There is a roaring torrent. It is what is,
> Your life, the dream of water going elsewhere.

Whenever I read one of Bill's poems—he has two collections, *Distances* and *Gone Haywire and other Old Sayings*—I can hear his voice, timbre, and rhythm, aware of the sources of many references, feel the existential tangles. The poems possess a depth far beyond the surface of the man I knew.

Like others I have heard from since Bill's death, I will miss him very much, perhaps more so because we shared so much in our lives, memories now left only to me.

NARCS

NOW THAT MANY STATES, eager for tax revenues and space in their prisons, are decriminalizing recreational marijuana or making medical marijuana accessible with a wink and a nod, it's a time warp to remember a period when just a few loose grains of weed could cause an uproar. But that's what happened in the late nineteen sixties during my second year on the campus where I ended up spending my teaching life.

For some reason—perhaps erratic steering—the police in nearby Morristown, New Jersey, pulled over a car in which a young student named Jackie was riding with her then-boyfriend. A search turned up a few escaped marijuana flecks in her coat pocket. No rolled joints, no weighable stash. Later I heard Jackie told people the original joint had been her boyfriend's. Did they share when it was lit, reclining the cars seats, leaning back and inhaling as their fingers passed the criminal object back and forth? Did they sigh and utter something like, "Groovy"?

The local narcotics force, then led by a man named Paul, concluded that Jackie's pocket must have been the tip of the iceberg, our campus infested by drug vipers, on the verge of reefer madness. Criminality must be exposed. Their strategy led to planting a narc—a young woman named Linda—in classes as an agent to gather inadvertent admissions from those in the rows around her. But Linda was not really a student—never admitted, never enrolled. She just looked like one.

Despite her ability to pass, Linda's clandestine cover didn't last long. Blown. Word spread rapidly. Everyone— students, staff, and faculty—knew about the blatant spying, the fuzz infiltration. Outrage and protest, but also defense of the ploy by some *in loco parentis* fans.

All the hallway fulminations culminated with a packed faculty assembly, students omitted, almost every member of our small, full-time teaching cohort present. The university's founding president, Peter, made his case. He had a duty to protect students. He trusted law enforcement. The police made a formal request, and he acceded. Anything the police wanted, he told the audience.

Back and forth the argument went, the room tense with alternating condemnation and support. I've rarely seen a faculty so animated over an issue other than parking. Finally, a vote was taken—endorse or oppose Peter's decision. He won 39 to 36. I've never forgotten those numbers.

I was an opposer, as were many of my English department colleagues, as might be expected from a group of people who read a lot, including males with beards. I also was the newly chosen president of our local AAUP (Association of American University Professors) chapter, that election being a formality because no one else wanted the job.

But it did give me a semblance of official standing and a TV interview with Reed Collins, a reporter for the nearby New York CBS station and a man who lived in town not far from the campus. He possessed a resonant announcer's voice, clearly an old hand at asking questions of novices like me. I managed not to grope and babble in my thirty-second reply, arguing that the heart of the issue was a matter of academic freedom, the privileged privacy of what was spoken during a class. In effect, what was said in the classroom should stay in the classroom.

I was considering what students might reveal during a discussion. Faculty words were fair game, open to note taking and public repetition by anyone who had been paying attention. Faculty were, however, protected—theoretically—by the standard of academic freedom that permitted written and spoken statements those in power might consider offensive and controversial.

Certain actions were another matter. Our campus crisis took place a few years after Timothy Leary, the LSD guru, was fired from Harvard for the official reason of not showing up to teach his scheduled classes—the real cause pressuring his graduate students to participate in psychedelic research and violating a university rule by including undergraduates. Leary exacerbated his malfeasance by also taking the drugs himself during the experiments. But Leary's famous phrase—*turn on, tune in, drop out*—became the mantra for a generation. Former President Richard Nixon called Leary "the most dangerous man in America."

Could Jackie, with the pot in her pocket, be considered a variation of that danger? Were Paul, Linda, and Peter working to save a generation from ruin?

When interviewed, I wasn't thinking of Leary or narcotic dangers, and I wasn't even sure if academic freedom applied to students. It probably doesn't. Still, in my experience, those in classes devoted to discussion of books or their own writings tend to be open and uninhibited. What if an unknowing student—Jackie and her like—had written an essay or a poem or a story based on being high? What if, during the discussion, others compared the words she used to describe her experience with those they would have chosen for theirs? What if Linda—a deceptive smile on her face—had been scribbling notes, naming names, reporting to Paul or others at headquarters? It's often hard enough to get students to talk in class. The threat of self-incrimination could lead to stony silence.

Linda, once her ruse was exposed, became useless, of course. But Paul's people were wiser the next time. They found a young man—tall, thin, and blond—named Mike who had been arrested for flying a weather balloon in an area not far from an airport. He was in legal trouble but could have charges dropped if he agreed to become an informant. This time a narc who was a legitimate student. But if I knew about Mike's role, how many others did? How effective could he be at exposing perpetrators? For that matter, how hard did he try?

A number of years after this ploy by county narcotics, a set of odd circumstances led to Paul and his
wife coming to my apartment for dinner. We enjoyed
a friendly reminiscence of the events, during which I
learned that Linda had moved to the Southwest for a
career in law enforcement and Paul admitted his efforts
to rid the campus of drugs had been ineffective.

He didn't have to tell me. The evidence had paraded
in front of my eyes, blatant, no subterfuge needed. I remember the ludes fad, when students semi-comatose on
downers could barely lift their heads from their desks.
I remember Teddy, who slept in his car most nights,
obviously too stoned to stagger off to a bed. I remember
Robyn, who waltzed into an office where my colleague
Neil and I were talking, her eyes wide and spinning,
chanting that she had just dropped acid and waltzing
out. Be careful, we told her, as if that meant anything.

Now we live in a time of fatal opioid overdoses,
communities devastated, parents dead in their cars,
their newly orphaned children bawling in the backseat.
In comparison, ludes and pot and acid seem benign,
excesses of a more innocent age. Clearly, the war on
drugs has been a rout, a wipeout by the hallucinatory
opposition. The fiasco of our long-ago campus skirmish
served as a straw in the wind.

And what of student privacy? That too seems a
quaint memory, what with self-exposure on Facebook
and YouTube, what with texts and tweets and other
posts, what with CCTV, what with commercial data

collection, what with criminal hacking.

Does vanished privacy contribute to today's student anxiety? The number of students in depression and despair has grown significantly in recent years, apparently replacing drugs as the primary threat to young people.

My own campus has acknowledged the crisis with new guidelines titled "Reporting Students of Concern," with this explanation: "Students might feel alone, isolated, helpless, and even hopeless. These feelings can easily disrupt academic performance and can result in harmful behaviors, including substance abuse and suicide attempts." Faculty and staff may possess a unique position of confidence, regarded as caring and trustworthy, more comfortable for students to open up to than family and friends.

If a student is considered to be in immediate danger, staff and faculty are advised to alert public safety. If the concern involves matters of behavior, health, wellness, missed classes, etc., contact should be made with the dean of students or counseling services.

Although these reporting guidelines seem to be voluntary, meetings all faculty and staff are obliged to attend—according of one source—make it seem mandatory. In fact, those running the meeting note that the university can be fined tens of thousands of dollars if it is discovered that someone had knowledge of something that they did not report but ended up badly. Lawsuits appear to be as much a concern for the university as student well-being. Such may be the reality for all universities now.

In effect, without even a physical search, shreds of peril have been discovered in the figurative coat pockets of a multitude of students, a generation of Jackies, the prototype who had never been in real danger. Unfortunately, today many are, turning all faculty and staff into a cadre of Linda narcs, alert for harmful behaviors, on guard to prevent the worst.

In retrospect, the days of Jackie, Linda, Paul, Peter, Tomothy, Mike, Teddy, Robyn, and all the qualude zonked students seem so innocent, a halcyon time of tie-dyes and love-ins and hazy dreams of a future of bliss.

TROLLEYOLOGY

A MORAL CONUNDRUM I've encountered in several variations involves a driverless, out-of-control trolley car hurtling down a track toward a group of waiting people who don't have time to get out of the way. But a short distance from that group a lone man stands at the edge of the platform. You—the person confronting the conundrum—have to make a split-second decision whether to save one or many. Push that man onto the rails to stop the trolley and, thereby, sacrifice his one life to preserve the several in the group. Or refuse to play God. (An entire ethical field, "trolleyology," is devoted to the dilemma.)

In the version I remember best, the person at the heart of our dilemma is a fat man, weighted with all the fat-shaming prejudices endemic to our culture. Those in the group are assumed to be above the self-indulgence that piles on pounds. While the obese man doesn't deserve death, the unstated implication is that his gluttonous life isn't as valuable as that of the assembled svelte and toned. Note, too, that he is alone beside the tracks, perhaps friendless and less likely to be missed than the bonded cohort. Yet, even if the one man—in an alternate version—had just come from the gym bearing presents for his loving children, would that change the fundamental issue of sacrificing one to save the many?

::

Transpose the dilemma to an analogous situation. The lone man is now a schizophrenic woman haunted by twisted fantasies and a burden to her husband and children. The group on the track is several hundred college professors, men and women with advanced degrees responsible for educating the future leaders of our society. The profs could be a bunch of egotistical snobs, all with abysmal student evaluations. While the stakes may not be who lives and who dies, the core of the choice still comes down to a choice between one or many.

That version of the moral conundrum was the one I faced when I was the chief negotiator for a faculty union on the final night of bargaining with the forces of the administration team. We were in a hotel on neutral territory near New Jersey's Garden State Parkway, miles from the campus, each side huddled to conspire in small bedrooms before the teams met formally in a conference room that smelled of tobacco and stale coffee. (This was back when people could still smoke in hotel rooms.)

Our faculty colleagues had voted to authorize a strike to wrest higher salaries and better teaching loads. Away from campus gossip, we—the representative team of eight—didn't know what wonders the faculty expected of us and what we could hope to accomplish. What really mattered? Yet collective bargaining is much like immersion in a sporting contest. The goal of winning releases adrenaline, even if the stakes were ultimately trivial.

Even in a climate-controlled facility, the emotional atmosphere in those hotel rooms was hothouse. We fretted, on edge, sleepless, pacing, trying to mindread the administration team, people we knew well transformed into the opposition, even though in just a few days after an agreement they would return to their normal status as compatible lunch companions.

Though I could take showers, I felt unwashed, while those around me on both sides looked as unwashed as I felt, even though I knew that they too bathed daily. Ours was a dirty business.

All along, I suspected I was in over my head, just a titular chief negotiator, no slick debater, certainly unconvincing as an authoritative shouter of demands. Strategy was my strength, behind-the-scenes writing of contract clauses. My friend Peter, a senior professor of mathematics, was the real force, I—at best—a front. Still, my responsibilities lay at the heart of the negotiating matter. Hundreds depended on me to deliver a welcome result.

So, where does the madwoman come in? She was my then-wife, Judy, assumed by me to be at home, sunken in a padded chair, chain smoking Marlboros, and vocalizing the words of the hallucinatory beings that haunted her brain. The way she spent every day, rarely eating, rarely sleeping.

That may sound bizarre. It is, in fact, bizarre. Few people have had the experience of living with a schizophrenic. But that had been my life for ten years, and my adolescent daughters and I were used to coping with it, existing around Judy's ghost-ridden presence, her minimal contact with us and our world, she much more fascinated by the warring voices that coaxed, shouted, cried, demanded in hers.

It's not that her initial breakdown and the progression from paranoia to full-blown psychosis hadn't been traumatic for the girls and me. When our daughters were born, babies in her arms, Judy made up songs for them, caressed their faces, touched fingertips to their fine hair. Then it stopped, not all at once, but over several months—no touching, no singing, no laughter, just meals slapped on a tabletop so that she could leave the kitchen and return to her terrors.

As young as the girls were at the beginning, they sensed their mother's increasing detachment into fearful self-absorption. For me, the first sign of the girls' upset was plunging grade school performance, one dropping from the highest reading group to the lowest in just weeks, the other assigned to special tutoring. Their self-images shattered. Shamed, they found a new set of friends from families troubled by alcohol and poverty. My daughters either avoided coming home or sat with fixed stares watching *The Brady Bunch* or *The Partridge Family*, anything but what acknowledging was happening in the rooms around them.

Initially, I expected professionals to intervene and restore Judy. Nothing succeeded. Her illness worsened. What had begun as fears that hostile neighbors were

bugging our house, that strangers in passing cars were
grave enemies, led to terror that the wrong choice of a
soup can in a supermarket would doom a family member, then to a belief that signs and messages everywhere
she looked were sending ominous messages to her alone.
Ultimately, those messages became internalized, a group
of authoritarian voices barraging her with commands.
Finally, I took the advice of a psychology colleague who
told me my choice was either give up on my schizophrenic wife or ruin three other people—my daughters
and me—in the fruitless attempt to save her. The trolley
conundrum.

::

Living with Judy had meant an almost daily con-
frontation with a berserk trolley, a constant demand for
reactions and decisions. Should I go into debt to pay for
a Freudian analyst I felt sure would be useless? Should I
move to a new town for a geographic cure I knew was
folly? (I did both.) Should I tell my young daughters how
sick their mother was? That predicament was yet another
delusion. How could they not know when they had witnessed so much, day by day. On one, just as we sat for
an attempt at a family Thanksgiving meal, Judy suddenly
grabbed the serving dish with the roasted turkey, ran to
the back door, and threw dish and bird into the yard,
screaming that it was poisoned.

How could they not know when they heard her
voices shouteing angry confrontations with each other,

or when she left the house to wander through the streets of our town, muttering to herself, drawing suspicious stares? It must have been awful to be her, no doubt even worse than it was to be her husband, her child, or her parents.

::

So I pretended to have a normal existence, plunging into a variety of activities (escapes?)—like planning lessons, grading papers, spending time with friends, even trying to learn tennis.

Collective bargaining, the absorption in conflicts, issues, and strategies, provided an ideal distraction. Despite all the stresses, pressures, anxieties, and doubts I faced in the hotel that night, it was a relief from enduring the mental disintegration of the woman I had chosen to marry, the mother of my children.

I recall a lunch table where I could not stop myself from revealing my distress through examples of Judy's behavior, a colleague unfamiliar with my situation asked incredulously, "Who *is* that woman?"

"His wife," another colleague answered for me.

The wife they referred to bore little resemblance to the Judy I first met or the one I had lived with in the early years of our marriage. Then she had brimmed with enthusiasm, very appealing, excitement in her gleaming dark eyes. When we met, I had been immediately attracted by her face. Many people, men and women, considered her beautiful. From the start, she had been

fervent in causes, picketing discrimination and protest-
ing war—marching with banners, distributing flyers,
joining groups, eager to fix the world. Really caring.
That Judy might even have thrown herself in front of
a berserk trolley.

::

My moral crisis exploded with the ringing of a tele-
phone. Not that I could hear it. The phone that rang
(this was before cellphones) was located in our team's
main room down the hallway. I had given the number to family—just in case—never expecting it to be
used. But when Sherm, a gangly physicist, shuffled to
my room in slippers and told me I had a call, I felt an
immediate panic, even before seeing the concern on his
face.

I entered the other room, my shirt tails hanging,
aware that others were trying not to star at me, and
picked up the receiver with hesitant fingertips, as if it
might shock.

"Yes," I said. Then I heard the voice of my then-
mother-in-law, speaking slowly, each word boldfaced.
"Judy. Is. Missing." Her daughter, my wife, had disappeared, once again, had walked out of the house after
dark and was nowhere to be found in the neighbor-
hood, off on yet another paranoid mission.

The out-of-control trolley was speeding down the
track. Should I rush home at a similar pace to search
God knows where, abandoning my obligation to several

hundred colleagues on this crucial night? Or should I remain to fulfill my bargaining role? Which duty should I choose?

I stood frozen and silent.

::

Through a cruel irony, in her psychosis Judy had become trapped by her need to solve the world's problems, fierce voices demanding that she set out on missions for the CIA, commands that drove her from the house and onto the street, where she began long walks from New Jersey to Washington, but never got far.

She carried a wallet with an ID, making it easy for policemen to know where she belonged when they found a disheveled, chain-smoking, fixed-eyed, muttering woman telling them she had been summoned to fulfill a secret government mission. I would fetch her from police stations, pleading with cops to take her to a psychiatric ward. Couldn't they see how sick she was? They wouldn't meet my eyes. They just shrugged. She hadn't broken any laws.

::

Although one might think a bunch of college professors involved in collective bargaining to be an aberration, far from the blue-collar norm of such negotiations, I learned that it's no different. As with any kind of bargaining—business or governmental—much posturing is required, decoy demands contrived to give up with breast-beating grimaces, moanings about how much pain their sacrifice is costing us. A smoke screen for what really mattered.

In truth, the formal sessions of two teams fulminating across from each other at a conference table is no more than empty theatrics. The actual decisions take place behind the scene, say, four people, two on each side, closeted away to focus on the real business, speaking calmly and seriously, hammering out the specifics. On this night, I was one of the two faculty—along with Peter—scheduled to be in that room, my presence essential.

I was also very much aware of the question of my competence, as in, *Who am I to take on such responsibility?* After all, I taught writing and literature, prepared to speak about point of view and Dickens. What did I know about the world of budgets and contract clauses?

My own shortcomings multiplied when the dilemma involved another matter even further beyond my capabilities, namely a psychotic wife. Yet, here I was, forced to choose among inadequacies.

Like the potential pusher of the fat man, my lips against the phone's mouthpiece, feeling of eyes of the others in that hotel room, I muttered my decision.

"Sorry," I told my ex-mother-in-law. "I can't leave the negotiations." Then I handed the phone back to Sherm and walked out the door.

::

I had my reasons. However much I actually could have rationalized in those few seconds, the trolley conundrum involves hypotheticals. The lone man, fat or buff, and the assembled group—prize-winning poets or a children's choir—are fictional concepts, representing one and many. In my case, I was dealing with real people I knew well and consequences that might resonate long after any imaginary impact.

One additional factor in my staying was the inertia of place. Place being the dislocation to a strange hotel where I had been immersed in the intense reality of the bargaining showdown, surrounded by colleagues, all of us breathing the same air of raw tension. It all felt—and was—unreal. This situational here and now absorbed me. Judy, on the other hand, was lost somewhere thirty miles and an hour away, her disappearance an intrusion. What would I do if I abandoned the bargaining? Drive aimlessly around dark streets in search of her familiar shape? No, I'd sit helplessly in a glum room with her parents, sharing silence, waiting for the authorities to call.

In that hotel on that climatic night, I knew I was playing some sort of game as much as I was engulfed by the goal of succeeding, making a heroic stand, scoring the winning points. By the weekend the adventure would have faded to a memory. But for Judy every moment, every action, was deadly serious, every step the edge of a fatal mistake. She clenched her jaw, ground her teeth, lit Marlboro after Marlboro.

For most of us, few of our concerns, regardless of importance, are actually matters of life and death. But for Judy they were, each moment a mortal crisis. If not life and death, decisions and disaster. Haunted and terrified day and night.

Unlike Judy, I had escapes—like involvement with bargaining—excuses to get away from the house and her, an ability to immerse myself in other realities like the classroom, conversations with colleagues, even tedious committee meetings. The relief of topics other than a crazy wife.

Then there was the shameful part of me, exacerbated by that phone call in the hotel, the guilty secret I swallowed day after day, the wish that Judy would vanish from my life. I couldn't speak it aloud, couldn't make myself imagine the actuality, knowing that her fate as a homeless crazy woman haunting strange streets would cause even greater misery than seeing her contained in our living room.

So, I stayed to play out my role as chief negotiator, up through the night, so absorbed in contractual minutia that I couldn't help but shut out thoughts of what might be happening in my real life, relegating my wife to the role of the fat man.

::

I still have the paperback of Albert Camus' *The Myth of Sisyphus and Other Essays* filled with her underlinings and marginal notations. At the bottom of page 91, after Camus' final sentence—"One must imagine Sisyphus happy"—she wrote in tiny script: "The search for meaning is enough of a principle to make life meaningful." I still find seeing those words heartbreaking, knowing that not long after she penciled them her life would become lost in meaninglessness.

In the end, Judy was found wandering just blocks from our house and brought back to her anxious parents waiting at our house. Meanwhile, we faculty had gotten pretty much the contract we wanted. But that wouldn't last. Future negotiations—with me no longer involved—produced several more contracts, any gains lost one by one, until the Supreme Court's Yeshiva decision declared that faculty in private universities were actually managers and, therefore, ineligible to negotiate for themselves as employees. No more bargaining. By the time our union was decertified, Judy had been institutionalized for five years. After five more years, she died of lung cancer from all that smoking. By then I had divorced her, another version of decertification.

I still have remorse, not about my decision to choose negotiations that night but, instead, about my inability to rescue the woman I married from madness. The trolley crashed. No decision I could have made in the hotel room that night would have saved her. Anyway, that's the conclusion I live with.

THE DAY ROBERT GRAVES SANG TO ME

For Bill Zander

THIS HAPPENED DECADES AGO, when Robert Graves was still alive, though far up in years, wearing his trademark stiff broad-brimmed black hat on a cobblestone street of Deya, Mallorca. It was Graves, of course, who made that Balearic island and that specific village a lure for expatriate writers and artists when he ran off with Laura Ryding in 1925 and stayed for several years. In 1946, he returned with his second wife, Beryl Hodge, and remained for the rest of his life, four decades, until his death in 1985. And why not? Beautiful scenery, ideal weather, brilliant flowers, the sparkling Mediterranean, low rent, cheap food, even cheaper wine. Even in Franco-era Spain, there was little not to like. In 1838, Chopin and George Sand founded their love nest in Valdemossa, on the road to Palma, the capital, where tourist buses gather for a whiff of illicit romance. In twentieth-century Deya, expatriates, bohemians, and sabbatical-freed academics gather to work at their arts.

Today the village is probably not much larger than it was when I visited at Christmas in 1972, with fewer than 700 inhabitants in 15 square kilometers, the smallest municipality on the island. The town is surrounded by rugged mountains, the highest, at 1064 meters (3500 feet), is Puig des Teix. Deya itself is 220 meters (720 feet) above sea level, and the story goes that Graves chose it because that altitude kept it "relatively free of mosquitoes."

I was reminded of that trip when, in a recent *New York Sunday Times* entertainment section, I saw two pieces by Jesse McKinley. He had been a towheaded toddler when I saw him in the Deya home of his father, James McKinley, a writer and past editor of *New Letters* at the University of Missouri-Kansas City. Another son, Jimmy, about ten then, was dispatched to get wine for the visitors. He's a *Times* reporter now too, at one point stationed in Africa, and his sister, Molly, the daughter, also works for the *Times*.

Before that trip the only other country I had been in besides the U.S. was England, where the alcohol laws were even more restrictive than those in the States. Once I had to drive for hours in Scotland to find a place for lunch because pubs wouldn't allow me inside with two underage daughters. So, it amazed me to see a young boy run out and fetch a bottle of the local red. But within a few days it became natural to watch a group of kids, mine included, swiveling on the stools of an outdoor tavern as they swigged Coca Cola and even, I learned later, sangria.

::

The trip to Mallorca came about because my friend and colleague, William Zander—poet, journalist, fisherman, hawk watcher—invited my family for the Christmas break, and I surprised him by accepting. Bill had taken a year to live in Spain with Lady Brett Ashley, his dog, to write his own poetry and learn idiomatic Spanish to translate poems of Antonio Machado. Before settling in Deya, he traveled throughout Spain, visiting a number of Machado's environs—Seville, Madrid, Soria, Baeza, Segovia. He mastered the language and the geography well enough to publish a number of his English versions of Machado's work.

The Spanish assumed Brett was a valuable animal. Why else would Bill spend so much money to bring her across an ocean? In fact, Brett was just a mutt, beagle-based, with a calm disposition and a host of frequent-flyer miles. In the Deya restaurant where groups of us gathered for four-course, one-dollar-fifty meals, she would sleep under the table and never beg.

Bill came to Deya because a mutual friend from Missouri suggested he get in touch with the McKinleys when in Spain. Among their kindnesses, they helped him find a cottage, in an outlying hamlet called Lluch Alcari, for about fifty dollars a month. It had two stories and several large rooms, but only one main fireplace in a small alcove. The temperature plunged with sundown, and so we huddled in that alcove while the dense olive wood logs glowed with a steady red heat. Bill did have a small stove in his bedroom where he burned small chips of olive wood, but he was too polite a host to abandon us to the chill.

Evening shivers were a minor nuisance when the late December days were so wonderful, bright with sun, comfortable in only a sweater. Mornings I would walk down a crooked path past a tethered goat with a clanking bell to sit on a rock and just gaze out at the Mediterranean.

::

Perhaps while I was out contemplating the sea, the writers who had chosen Deya for long-term residence were busy at their pads and typewriters satisfying the day's creative urges before an evening of socializing over food and wine. In such a setting everything was art—the landscape, the rugged stone buildings, the sky, the water, the food, the drink.

Robert Graves? Actually, I only met him for a minute, though an Englishman named Martin Tallents held British teas every afternoon and Graves, despite his years as an expatriate, was a regular attendee. Bill, once connected by Jim McKinley, had a standing invitation, and so knew Graves. Our encounter took place in front of the town *estanco*, the government store that sold tobacco and stamps and served as the village post office. As Bill and I approached with my daughters Jenny, then nine, and Pamela, then ten, Graves came by, unshaven, dressed in his black costume, his face as craggy as the surrounding hills, his thick white hair under a small straw hat. When he saw us, he stopped to tip that hat.

"Robert," Bill said, "I'd like you to meet my friends from New Jersey."

Graves then broke into a dance step and sang a song about New Jersey that I had never heard before and have never heard since. But he knew it by heart.

Pamela recalls the moment vividly "because he was the first famous person I ever met." Recently, she attended a Robert Bly male-bonding presentation with a friend and, while Bly was signing a book for the friend, told him she had run into another poet named Robert on Mallorca. "You met Robert Graves," he said. "I'm jealous."

Back then, outside the *estanco*, Jenny suddenly asked Graves, "How many books have you written?" which was strange for her because she had never seemed interested in authors.

"One hundred and thirty-eight," he told her.

"That's a lot!" She was impressed, and so was I.

LIVING IN HISTORY

I LIVED IN THE TITHE BARN in Oxfordshire for six months. I lived in the Turf House in New Jersey for twenty-two years. I spent many hours in my office in the Florham Mansion, where I taught for more than fifty years. I slept in several different bedrooms in Wroxton Abbey in Oxfordshire, where I taught for short periods over fifteen years. That doesn't include rooms occupied during brief stays of European travel—along the Rhine, in the Swiss Alps, on a Tuscan Farm, on the Grand Canal, in a Hebrides hotel, to name just a few. In each of these places I was very conscious of being immersed in history, some just a century or two, some many hundreds of years. Now in the epilogue of my life, downsized to a unit in a relatively new apartment complex constructed on the site of a quarry, I wonder how much of that past, both mine and world's, will survive me—Venice constantly flooded, saltwater eating at monumental foundations, Notre Dame teetering, Australia on fire, glaciers melting, seas rising, species dying. My own future is clearly short term, that of the world as we have known is seriously questionable. This danger makes me even more aware how fortunate I've been to enjoy such a close association with the continuities of the past. My memories are rich.

The Tithe Barn

That was my home—my actual mail address—in an Oxfordshire village called Church Hanborough during my first sabbatical leave, found by placing an ad in the Oxford *Mail*, replied to by a sculptor named Steve Hurst, who had converted half the barn into living quarters for his family, planning to turn the other half into a studio. But he had a teaching job in London and a home in Putney. And so, he sought renters while the barn pended.

Our bedroom windows overlooked the village cemetery, weathered stones with eroding letters. I could make out a number of Lees, a family that had been in the village for many generations, its descendants at the time an elderly couple who ran the tiny shop and post office just across the street. We also looked out at the never-locked church of Saint Peter and Paul with a steeple that rose high behind the headstones.

It was Penelope Liveley who told me about the church, the fact that its entrance doorway dated from the 1100s and that the posted list of priests and vicars went back to church's beginning, the initial priests bearing just one name. Penelope was our neighbor, living in the converted rectory with her husband, Jack, then a politics don at St. Peters College, Oxford. She was writing young adult novels of Cotswold history, at the time before she became a major British novelist and a Booker Prize winner.

Her sense of history was so unlike mine, with my American sense of what amounted to the past. For her, the village pub was "new," merely eighteenth century. I do recall her annoyance when Steve, our landlord, had the roof slates replaced on the Tithe Barn's residential half. The old original Stonesfield slates lay in random heaps on the dirt, offered to anyone who would cart them away. For Penelope, they represented objects of historical value, and I understood, a convert to preserving the past.

My daughters in the local primary school were certainly learning about the history all around them, the British curriculum very different from that of their American, Dick and Jane grammar school. In England, they were in the first and second years of junior school, writing research papers on topics like—for the older— the French Montgolfier Brothers, the first humans to cross the English Channel in a hot air balloon. When the younger was studying the Romans in Britain, we drove a half-hour to the remains of the Chedworth Roman Villa, mainly foundations and a few wall portions. At eight, she was able to explain the process of the bath—the warming up rooms and the cooling down. I hadn't known that, nor about the Channel balloon.

The day we went to Stonehenge became an adventure, the fan belt of my old Hillman Minx snapping just as we reached the crest of a hill outside the town of Amesbury, the stones in sight, coasting down to the parking lot, me having to walk back to the town to find an open garage and a mechanic who would drive me back with a fresh belt. Still, we were able to roam among the stones without barriers. Since then I've been absorbed in the mystery of how such massiveness got there from their origins in Wales.

The Minx replaced with a rented Renault Four, I experienced much of England's past—castles, cathedrals, ruins, estates. They were all around. Centuries of them, Blenheim Palace just down the road from the Tithe Barn.

The Turf House

No doubt the Turf House in Florham Park, New Jersey, would have been dismissed by Penelope as merely eighteenth century, new. It's first half was built circa 1790 when George Washington was president, not long after General Cornwallis' English surrender at Yorktown. The second half went up in 1808 when Jefferson was president. The house goes back to the literal beginnings of American history even though that history is still a newcomer for the world.

Before we sold and moved—actually one reason we sold—a group of condominiums were constructed on the land behind the house, and over the months I could watch the stages of construction, the Komatsu earth diggers carving out foundations, long trucks dropping off beams and lumber, cranes lifting preconstructed Pella windows and bundled roofing shingles. The more I understood the need for these heavy machines, the more I appreciated the efforts of the men who built the Turf House.

Not only did they have to shovel out the space for the foundation by brute labor, they had to cut down and trim trees for beams and planks and lathing, grind a mixture of seashells and horsehair to fill in walls, and forge nails to secure the wood, although in some areas the beams were locked together with pegs.

The roof rafters were cut from a variety of trees, the bark still on them—but petrified. In fact, much of the original wood was petrified. One day, as I looked on, a worker with a powerful electric professional carpenter's drill tried to bore into a beam. After a quarter of an inch, the bit shattered.

The flooring of the second story was the original bird's eye maple, hand-hewn planks of varying widths, some with knotholes that the sisters who grew up in the house used to drop notes for the future. The door latches and hinges were original forgings, the kind seen in British period dramas. Many of the windows panes were still filled with old, bubbled glass.

When we purchased the house, we were able to get copies of the surveys going back to 1800 from the country offices. Any before that were locked away who knows where in the state capital. Up until 1923, they were handwritten, perhaps with quill pens at one stage, with the s's looking like f's. The builder was a man named Barzillia Campfield, who was responsible for many of the homes in the area. According to the surveys the property shrank over the decades, sold off at the edges, down to a half acre when we lived there.

The name Turf House—a designation unusual for any American community where homes are identified by street number—came from its function in the early nineteenth century, when a man named James Woodruff purchased the property. Originally, like others in the community, he created straw brooms in the house, effectively participating in a cottage industry. But the coming of mass factory broom production overwhelmed the small makers. Woodruff needed an alternative income. He took his cue from the Irish workers he had watched building a turnpike through the area in 1817, when they discovered peat bogs in the surrounding wetlands. The Irish had long dried brick-sized blocks of peat—*turf* in America—for fireplace fuel in cold weather. Woodruff followed suit and stored the turf in the house's attic, selling it from a horse-drawn cart and giving the house its name. That wasn't his life's career though. He gave up turf to become a journalist and local historian for a newspaper called *The Jerseyman*. But the name stuck with the house.

When maintaining the house became too much for us, we feared it would be demolished like many of the structures around it. Luxury condos loomed behind us. The buildings on the block across the street became heaps of rubble in preparation for an apartment complex. Our realtor told us the likely fate of the Turf

House was a teardown. Fortunately, we found a buyer who was a Colonial history buff and a long-time admirer of the house, committed to preserving it in some form for the future. That was a happy surprise. We live in a country with minimal interest in saving its physical past, not if the land can be turned to immediate profit. To that end, almost all the town's other Campfield houses have vanished.

Florham

The entire Florham estate in Morris County, New Jersey, almost went the way of the Barzillia Campfield houses, although it occupied more than one thousand acres, featuring a one-hundred-and-ten-room mansion (originally one of the ten largest private homes in America) designed by the firm of McKim, Mead & White, with the trees, landscaping, and garden designed by the firm of Frederick Law Olmsted. It had been the country home of the Vanderbilt-Twomblys, a marriage between two of the country's wealthiest families. The estate offered several other architecturally significant buildings, with the details of woodworking, stonework, and ornaments the achievements of master craftsmen. It was a monument to Gilded Age magnificence. But no heirs wanted it, including the surviving Twombly daughter and her two sons. Like the other estates and great houses that once had filled the area, Florham had become a white elephant, too expensive to maintain, the property potentially more valuable if converted to commercial uses.

Florham was threatened with the demolition that obliterated most of its fellows, on the verge of being turned into a setting for streets of small homes that would have added eight thousand people to the local population, overwhelming schools and services. Fortunately, Fairleigh Dickinson University, in the midst of an enrollment boom, chose Florham for the site of a new campus.

That saved the historic buildings and the close to two hundred landscaped acres. The rest of the land—the Florham Farm—had already been sold to ESSO, later EXXON, for offices and research facilities. When EXXON merged with Mobile and left town, that property eventually became home to a New York Jets training facility, the U.S. headquarters of BASF, two medical buildings, a hotel, an apartment building, and most recently a development of more than two hundred single homes and condominiums. What had once been an exemplary farm with herds of prizewinning Guernsey cattle is now a source of profits and traffic jams.

Throughout the half-century that I walked the grounds and the gardens of Florham, taught classes in many rooms that had housed guests and family, had my own office in what had been the mansion's women servants' quarters, explored nooks and crannies of the land and buildings, I was keenly aware that the likes of me would never have been allowed into the great house, where visitors had arrived in horse-drawn carriages, Rolls Royces, or a private rail car, dressed for gourmet dinners and midnight dancing, and strolled the gardens in their finery. Legend has it that Florence Vanderbilt Twombly hid servants with rakes behind bushes to smooth out the stones in front of the mansion to immediately erase tire tracks and the grooves of carriage wheels. At best, I might have been one of those secreted servants, gazing at the massive entrance door with little idea of the elegance within.

Yet, parvenu that I was, I spent about the same number of years at Florham as Mrs. Twombly and came to know much of its history, participating in the writing of five books on its creation, its high society functions, and its conversion to a college campus. That conversion is what allows Florham to exist today, still echoing some of the glories of its past, when so many other estates in the area and throughout the country are the sites of residential rows, office complexes, and parking lots, their glory no more than old photographs and fading memories.

Wroxton Abbey

This great Oxfordshire mansion, home to Lord Norths for many centuries, also came close to a Campfield house fate in the mid-twentieth century, a period when more than one thousand others too costly to maintain British mansions were demolished. While Florham spent only three years in limbo, Wroxton endured thirty. The last Lord North had died childless in his late nineties in 1933 with no direct heirs. Like the Twombly relatives, no similar North connections wanted the burden of so many rooms and so many acres. The estate reverted to Trinity College, Oxford, to which the college's founder, Sir Thomas Pope, had endowed the property in 1556, with a provision that allowed his descendants to occupy it as long that they existed as a family.

The designation *abbey* is a misnomer because the original building was actually a priory created in 1216-1217, although ownership of a manor at Wroxton was recorded in 1089. A year after Henry VIII dissolved monasteries in 1536, the land and ruins were purchased by Sir Thomas Pope, treasurer of Henry's Court of Augmentations. Perhaps Henry amused himself with the fact that he substituted a Pope for a Pope. While the present estate is just sixty acres, the original holdings went on for miles and miles.

Thomas Pope never lived there. It was his nephew Sir William who built a mansion on the site in the early seventeenth century. Slates in the great hall and basement, as well as arches and doorway in the basement, date back to the early 1200 and 1300s. Like many other homes of its size, it wasn't completed in just one go. The final addition, adding another one-third to the building, didn't take place until the nineteenth century. The Norths took over in 1672 when a daughter of the final Pope, who left no male heir, married Francis North.

No heir of any gender in the twentieth century meant the end of the Norths. After the return of the abbey in the 1930s, Trinity College leased it to London clothiers Pawson & Leafs, which used it to keep its inventory safe from Nazi bombings of the city, ladies undergarments stacked in the Regency Room (made elegant for a visit of the Prince Regent), King James' bedroom stacked with bookkeeping ledgers. In 1948, the war over, the Abbey was leased to Lady Pearson, who divided it into rental apartments and opened a tearoom. The project failed financially as well as causing physical damage to the property.

In 1963, eight years after it purchased Florham, Fairleigh Dickinson University bought Wroxton from Trinity—the second great estate the university preserved from destruction—and began the costly process of restoration and conversion into the very first European campus owned by an American university. To rub salt in old wounds, Frederick Lord North had been George III's Prime Minister between 1770 and 1782, when Britain lost the Revolutionary War to the Colonies. The upstarts had taken over.

Changes to Wroxton were much more restricted than those to Florham because the abbey is listed as a Grade One historical property in England, the most significant preservation category, meaning any alterations must be carefully vetted before approval, if approved at all. For example, the roof in disrepair had to be restored with the original Stonefield slate at a very great expense, along with strict standards for finials, chimneys, and stone facing. When the mullions of the carriage house window began to rot, they couldn't be replaced with new wood but were required treatment with a chemical that would harden the old wood to make it usable.

My own ten-day Abbey stays in various bedrooms ranged over fifteen years of January MFA program residencies, a time of the year when the sun rises late and sets early. A number of much more significant guests had preceded me, including Kings James I and Charles I, whose names are noted outside the rooms they slept in, as well as the Queen's Room next door, where their wives stayed. Later in history, though not at the same time, Henry James and Theodore Roosevelt slept in one of the larger bedrooms. James praised the Abbey: "Everything that in the material line can render life noble and charming has been gathered into it with a profusion which makes the whole place a monument of past opportunity." I agree, though not in so many words.

Rooted in the Past

The history I know and have experienced has nothing to do with me as a person beyond a vicarious connection. I observed and enjoyed, but what I've learned and where I've been is all external. Perhaps it's an antidote to my personal history, which is random and rootless. The places I've lived in provide the satisfactions of associations with something much larger than myself and my limited life, a connection to more significant patterns. Unhappily, a threat to that history looms. The homes I've lived in, despite all they embody, are just physical structures, prey to—using the word associated with Henry VIII—dissolution. Potential rubble and ruin. The past is fragile, so much of it already vanished, inevitably more to follow. I'm fortunate in experiences that matter so much to me no matter what awaits us.

ALL I DIDN'T KNOW

I STILL HAVE VIVID MEMORIES of riding on a bus down a central street of Metuchen, New Jersey, when I was eighteen and floundering. It was a short trip I took often, each time looking out at the large houses set back on sweeping lawns with manicured shrubbery, some with circular driveways and wide, pillared porticos, some with balconies and gleaming oriel windows. Each time I realized how little I knew about the people who occupied such grand homes. I couldn't even begin to guess at what their lives were like, aware how constrained my own life was, so limited I wasn't even able to conjure possibilities.

At the time I was a college sophomore, the few things I owned stored in a closet and metal dresser in the fraternity house attic where I slept on one of eight beds. My weekend home was the two-bedroom apartment my two sisters shared, fifteen minutes from the campus on that bus route. After our mother had died the year before, my sisters sold the small house I had grown up in and decided to rent in a town closer to my campus, and on a faster train line to their jobs.

That small house was one of three I had lived in in the town that had been my world, a limited place, self-contained, the people getting by in modest homes crammed on narrow streets The children were my schoolmates, kids with limited ambitions and expectations. When very young, we played random baseball and football games on vacant lots. When teens, we fixated over cars. I was dismal at sports, in a carless family, buying *Hot Rod* and *Motor Trend* to be able to join the conversations. School bored me, as it did the others, though I picked paperbacks from a rotating metal rack in a corner candy store, gathering a fifty-cent library but telling no friends about my reading because books mattered little to them.

Essentially, mine was just one of the standard little lives of the town, limited to the street routes I had taken day after day to schools and shops and playing lots and the houses of friends. We didn't expect more, had no idea what the more was that we could aspire to.

Their bread-earning parents, mainly fathers, whether they wore white shirt or blue collars, worked in low-level jobs, a few running small businesses, coming home to putter in their yards, paint their shutters, walk dogs, change their cars' oil, watch ball games on black and white TV sets. I have no idea whether they were content with their lives. My sense is that they just existed from day to day, not even realizing contentment was a question to be pondered. Perhaps in moments of three a.m. sleeplessness they fell into a deep brooding that vanished with the alarm clatter that signaled yet another day ahead behind a desk or a counter or a drill or lathe.

My classmates didn't talk much about futures, the

males expecting to finish high school and gravitate into jobs like their fathers' after a few years in the military, the females knowing they would serve milkshakes or ring cash registers for a few years until marriage and babies, often while still in their teens.

Only a handful of those in my high school graduating class went on to college, mainly because of their own version of inertia. Mine too. It was just expected that we would. We never had conversations about the schools we were applying to or what we would major in. Unlike today's generation of multiple applications, campus visits, SAT prep, anguish over rankings, we went by rote. I applied to only one college, Rutgers, the one my older brother had gone to, never exploring or considering options, never even bothering to wonder what else was out there.

Perhaps I'm being presumptuous about the people who surrounded me, projecting my own limited imagination of the time. But I don't think so. A list of classmate addresses compiled for a high school reunion decades later revealed the great majority hadn't gravitated far from our hometown, some just to a neighboring community.

Was I unique riding in that bus at eighteen, stung with the awareness of my vast ignorance of people and possibilities? I do recall sitting in classrooms and in that fraternity attic, my confusions preying at me, and saying to myself, "I'm really out of it," but having no notion of how to get with it.

The same autopilot that landed me at Rutgers guided me into the same fraternity my brother had been in years before. I think the members were amused by my legacy status. How could they turn me down? At the time the college was male-only and fraternities the norm. It was easy to get into one.

My fraternity changed my life, though it did take a number of years to realize how much. My wife, Alison, and I have often reviewed the unplanned decisions of our lives that have worked out so positively, the many times we had no idea what would happen next. She wonders why we've been so fortunate, including the circumstances that brought us together. I think of it as blundering into success. Carl Jung called such outcomes serendipity, "an unsought, unintended, and/or unexpected, but fortunate, discovery." My goal at the time was to be like most of the other freshmen and pledge a frat, though in my case—as with the college I attended—I didn't even think to choose between options.

My fraternity brothers came from backgrounds not unlike mine and that of my high school classmates. Their fathers were housepainters, chicken farmers, butchers, cigar store owners—some variety of working class. The crucial difference from the people in my town was that these sons possessed clear ambitions, plans for their futures. They expected very different lives from those of their parents as they pursued their pre-med, pre-law, and pre-professional curricula. And, for the most part, they achieved, some not only becoming physicians but teaching in med schools themselves or serving as a CEO of a major hospital or becoming a co-discoverer of gene splicing. Another achieved prominence as an award-winning academic. The lawyers worked with major clients and cases. The eventual corporate executives rose to positions like senior vice president of a worldwide pharmaceutical company.

Of course, I had no inkling of their futures when we listened to Dave Brubeck and Harry Belafonte records, sang drinking songs at Saturday night parties, concocted parade floats, and had our annual dining room food fight. Just a group of eighteen to twenty-two-year-olds, some in love, some randomly dating, some cutting classes for bridge games, but eager to learn. Those just a few years ahead of me explained what I should know, the books I should read, the courses I should take. They harangued me to abandon my originally intended journalism major. One even took the initiative to get me a full-tuition scholarship.

Still, unlike them, I lacked a career goal, had only a vague idea of what I wanted to do with my life. Advertising seemed like a possibility, an opportunity to come with clever slogans and wear tweeds. But Madison Avenue didn't want me, a fortunate rejection in the long run. Still, I was engaged and needed to earn a living to support a wife, so ended up as an advertising and sales trainee at General Electric in Schenectady. That was the first time I had a real job other than summer resort busboy or bookstore cashier or pin boy.

I didn't like it, not so much the eight-to-five routine as the vision of the years ahead, the programmed series of promotions up the managerial ranks, the higher salaries, the bigger offices. I saw what the executives did through their days, and it all looked empty and tedious. To have a meaningful life, I read much in my off hours and tried to write fiction. For the first time I formulated a plan for the future. I would apply to graduate school—something I had never even considered before—after I finished my six-month national guard training, with no clue whether I would be accepted, but without a backup plan. No matter, I had made a choice, elected to jump off the treadmill of the expected.

Serendipity again. Several graduate programs accepted me in spite of my undistinguished college record. But what I really wanted was the Iowa Writers' Workshop. Someone on the admissions committee must have flipped a coin in my favor. For several years I associated with the creative equivalents of my undergraduate fraternity brothers—people destined for significance in their careers, this time literary rather than medical, legal, or corporate. They won prizes, even became Poet Laureate. I hung out with my betters, earning degrees but no creative achievements. That took another decade.

The people I came to know at Rutgers and Iowa put me in touch with the prospects of a wider world, hints of possibilities, inklings of what's out there. I was no longer the bewildered kid on the bus, with no idea of what lay outside the window by my seat. Now, through obsessive reading and talking, I learned much about the past—lives and places, history and ideas, the range of human imagination.

While I had finally grown to a stage where I must make choices and weigh options, I still had little idea where those choices would take me, what would come next. Luckily, I benefitted from serendipity again, taking a teaching position in my home state but in a place nothing like the town I grew up in, once more enjoying happy associations with compatible colleagues and avoiding the meanness of academic egotism. These were people who had come from many diverse places. Their example made me want to travel, see more and more. Far more than the homes lining one street in one town.

That travel turned out to be another serendipitous turning point. I managed to make many trips, at least one a year, first to England again and again, until my wife, Alison—who shared and encouraged my passion for travel—suggested I was in a rut. An so we experienced much of Europe: Paris, Rome, Zurich, Prague, the Bernese Alps, the Tuscan hills, the Isle of Mull, and much more. People and places, castles and cathedrals, mountains and rivers, immersion in centuries of history.

Ultimately, after many decades, in the final years of living, I know what's out there, options beyond my economic grasp that I wouldn't want even if I could afford them. I've been in luxury apartments, five-star hotels, classy resorts, famous theatres, perfect villages, spectacular cities. I've known many of the world's more significant writers, physicians and scientists, world-class academics, corporate leaders, people of great wealth. I'm hardly one of them. But that's not the point. I've overcome the vast human unknown I felt on that bus. It's the knowing that matters to me, the assurance that I'm not missing the possibilities, free from regrets, wanting nothing that I haven't had, certain of what I didn't want and will never miss.

Still, I have yet to face the greatest unknown, the near future when time's winged chariot sweeps me off the face of the earth and I stare out into a dark vastness that has nothing to do with the travels or the potentials or the achievements of this life. My ultimate ignorance.